TEACHER'S PET PUBLICATIONS

LITPLAN TEACHER PACK
for
Frankenstein
based on the book by
Mary Shelley

Written by
Mary B. Collins

© 1995 Teacher's Pet Publications
All Rights Reserved

This **LitPlan** for Mary Shelley's
Frankenstein
has been brought to you by Teacher's Pet Publications, Inc.

Copyright Teacher's Pet Publications 1995

Only the student materials in this unit plan (such as worksheets, study questions, and tests) may be reproduced multiple times for use in the purchaser's classroom.

For any additional copyright questions,
contact Teacher's Pet Publications.

www.tpet.com

TABLE OF CONTENTS - *Frankenstein*

Introduction	5
Unit Objectives	7
Reading Assignment Sheet	8
Unit Outline	9
Study Questions (Short Answer)	13
Quiz/Study Questions (Multiple Choice)	21
Pre-reading Vocabulary Worksheets	37
Lesson One (Introductory Lesson)	53
Nonfiction Assignment Sheet	56
Oral Reading Evaluation Form	59
Writing Assignment 1	61
Writing Assignment 2	64
Writing Assignment 3	71
Writing Evaluation Form	62
Vocabulary Review Activities	72
Extra Writing Assignments/Discussion ?s	66
Unit Review Activities	76
Unit Tests	79
Unit Resource Materials	111
Vocabulary Resource Materials	125

A FEW NOTES ABOUT THE AUTHOR
MARY W. SHELLEY

SHELLEY, Mary Wollenstonecraft (Godwin) 1797-1851 Mary Shelley was born on August 30, 1797, in London, England. She was the daughter of a politically radical, literary couple who married just a few months before her birth to protect her legal status. Her father, William Godwin, was a philosopher and writer. Her mother, Mary Wollenstonecraft Godwin, author of *A Vindication of the Rights of Women*, was well-known for her feminist views. Mary never knew her mother, as she died a few days after giving birth. Mary Shelley received no formal early education. Instead, she was taught at home by her father. She listened to discussions by literary talents of the time, and read from her father's large library. As a child, she also enjoyed writing and daydreaming. At the age of fifteen she was sent to live in Scotland.

When she was seventeen, Mary eloped to France with noted poet Percy Bysse Shelley. Percy Shelley was, at that time, still married to his first wife, and the father of two small children. Their scandalous act was not approved of in English society.

Mary and Percy Shelley spent the summer of 1816 in Switzerland, and were neighbors of Lord Byron. It was during this time that she began writing *Frankenstein*. They were married in January of 1817, just a few weeks after Shelley's first wife committed suicide. On March 11, 1818, *Frankenstein* was published anonymously. The book received mixed reviews. Mary and Percy Shelley had five children in eight years, although only the last child, Percy Florence Shelley, lived to adulthood.

Also in March, 1818, the couple moved to Italy because of Percy Shelley's poor health. It was during this year that two of the children died. In 1822, Percy Shelley was sailing his boat when he was lost in a storm at sea. His body was found a few days later.

After her husband's death, Mary Shelley and her son returned to England. By that time her second novel, *Valperga*, and a dramatic adaptation of Frankenstein were both gaining in popularity. In 1824 she edited *Posthumous Poems,* a collection by Percy Shelley. She continued writing articles and stories for *Westminster Review,* the *Keepsake,* and other periodicals, editing Percy Shelley's works, and writing her own novels. In this way she was able to support herself and her son. Her other works include *History of a Six Weeks' Tour,* 1817; *Valperga,* or the *Life and Adventures of Castruccio, Prince of Lucca,* 1823; *The Last Man,* 1826; *The Fortunes of Perkin Warbeck,* 1830; *Rambles in Germany and Italy,* 1844; and *The Choice: A Poem on Shelley's Death,* edited by H. B. Forman, 1876. Several volumes of her letters were published after her death.

When her son married in 1848, Mary went to live with him and his wife. She lived a quiet life, and died on February 1. 1851.

In the years since Mary Shelley first wrote *Frankenstein,* there have been many adaptations, editions with illustrations by different artists, and critiques. Since 1910 many movies dealing with the *Frankenstein* theme have been made.

INTRODUCTION

This unit has been designed to develop students' reading, writing, thinking, and language skills through exercises and activities related to *Frankenstein* by Mary Shelley. It includes fifteen lessons, supported by extra resource materials.

The **introductory lesson** introduces students to the characteristics of the gothic novel. They will also be asked to complete a KWL sheet.

The **reading assignments** are approximately thirty pages each; some are a little shorter while others are a little longer. Students have approximately 15 minutes of pre-reading work to do prior to each reading assignment. This pre-reading work involves reviewing the study questions for the assignment and doing some vocabulary work for 8 to 10 vocabulary words they will encounter in their reading.

The **study guide questions** are fact-based questions; students can find the answers to these questions right in the text. These questions come in two formats: short answer or multiple choice The best use of these materials is probably to use the short answer version of the questions as study guides for students (since answers will be more complete), and to use the multiple choice version for occasional quizzes. It might be a good idea to make transparencies of your answer keys for the overhead projector.

The **vocabulary work** is intended to enrich students' vocabularies as well as to aid in the students' understanding of the book. Prior to each reading assignment, students will complete a two-part worksheet for approximately 8 to 10 vocabulary words in the upcoming reading assignment. Part I focuses on students' use of general knowledge and contextual clues by giving the sentence in which the word appears in the text. Students are then to write down what they think the words mean based on the words' usage. Part II gives students dictionary definitions of the words and has them match the words to the correct definitions based on the words' contextual usage. Students should then have an understanding of the words when they meet them in the text.

After each reading assignment, students will go back and formulate answers for the study guide questions. Discussion of these questions serves as a **review** of the most important events and ideas presented in the reading assignments.

After students complete extra discussion questions, there is a **vocabulary review** lesson which pulls together all of the fragmented vocabulary lists for the reading assignments and gives students a review of all of the words they have studied.

Following the reading of the book, two lessons are devoted to the **extra discussion questions/writing assignments**. These questions focus on interpretation, critical analysis and personal response, employing a variety of thinking skills and adding to the students' understanding of the novel. These questions are done as a **group activity**. Using the information they have acquired so far through individual work and class discussions, students get together to further examine the text and to brainstorm ideas relating to the themes of the novel.

The group activity is followed by a **reports and discussion** session in which the groups share their ideas about the book with the entire class; thus, the entire class gets exposed to many different ideas regarding the themes and events of the book.

There are three **writing assignments** in this unit, each with the purpose of informing, persuading, or having students express personal opinions. The first assignment is to write directions for performing a task. After this assignment is completed, the teacher will hold individual writing conferences to assess the students' work. The second writing assignment is to take the position of either prosecution or defense in the trial of Justine Moritz. In the third writing assignment students are asked to describe their ideas about having and being a friend.

In addition, there is a **nonfiction reading assignment**. Students are required to read a piece of nonfiction related in some way to *Frankenstein*. After reading their nonfiction pieces, students will fill out a worksheet on which they answer questions regarding facts, interpretation, criticism, and personal opinions. During one class period, students make **oral presentations** about the nonfiction pieces they have read. This not only exposes all students to a wealth of information, it also gives students the opportunity to practice **public speaking**.

The **review lesson** pulls together all of the aspects of the unit. The teacher is given four or five choices of activities or games to use which all serve the same basic function of reviewing all of the information presented in the unit.

The **unit test** comes in two formats: all multiple choice-matching-true/false or with a mixture of matching, short answer, and composition. As a convenience, two different tests for each format have been included.

There are additional **support materials** included with this unit. The **resource sections** include suggestions for an in-class library, crossword and word search puzzles related to the novel, and extra vocabulary worksheets. There is a list of **bulletin board ideas** which gives the teacher suggestions for bulletin boards to go along with this unit. In addition, there is a list of **extra class activities** the teacher could choose from to enhance the unit or as a substitution for an exercise the teacher might feel is inappropriate for his/her class. **Answer keys** are located directly after the **reproducible student materials** throughout the unit. The student materials may be reproduced for use in the teacher's classroom without infringement of copyrights. No other portion of this unit may be reproduced without the written consent of Teacher's Pet Publications, Inc.

UNIT OBJECTIVES *Frankenstein*

1. Through reading Shelley's *Frankenstein*, students will analyze characters and their situations to better understand the themes of the novel.

2. Students will demonstrate their understanding of the text on four levels: factual, interpretive, critical and personal.

3. Students will identify the characteristics of the gothic horror story.

4. Students will practice reading aloud and silently to improve their skills in each area.

5. Students will enrich their vocabularies and improve their understanding of the book through the vocabulary lessons prepared for use in conjunction with it.

6. Students will answer questions to demonstrate their knowledge and understanding of the main events and characters in *Frankenstein.*.

7. Students will practice writing through a variety of writing assignments.

8. The writing assignments in this unit are geared to several purposes:
    a. To check the students' reading comprehension
    b. To make students think about the ideas presented by the novel
    c. To make students put those ideas into perspective
    d. To encourage logical thinking
    e. To provide an opportunity to practice good grammar and improve students' use of the English language.

9. Students will read aloud, report, and participate in large and small group discussions to improve their public speaking and personal interaction skills.

READING ASSIGNMENT SHEET - *Frankenstein*

Date to be Assigned	Chapters	Completion Date
	Introduction, Preface, Letters	
	Chapters 1-5	
	Chapters 6-9	
	Chapters 10-15	
	Chapters 16-20	
	Chapters 21-24	

UNIT OUTLINE - *Frankenstein*

1 Introduction Distribute Materials PV Introduction	2 Read Introduction Study??	3 PVR 1-5 Oral Reading Evaluation	4 Quiz 1-5 PVR 6-9	5 Writing Assignment #1
6 Study ?? 6-9 PVR 1015	7 Study ?? 10-15 PVR 16-20	8 Study ?? 16-20 Writing Assignment #2	9 Writing Conference	10 PVR 21-24
11 Study ?? 21-24	12 Writing Assignment #3	13 Library Work	14 Vocabulary Review	15 Group Work
16 Movie and Discussion	17 Non-fiction Assignments	18 Review	19 Test	20

Key: P = Preview Study Questions   V = Vocabulary Work   R = Read

STUDY GUIDE QUESTIONS

SHORT ANSWER STUDY GUIDE QUESTIONS *Frankenstein*

Introduction, Preface, Letters
1. Why did Mary Shelley write *Frankenstein*?
2. What discussions influence the development of her idea?
3. In the preface, what does the author say she is trying to preserve?
4. What is the structure, or form, of the novel?
5. Who is writing the letters?
6. To whom are the letters written?
7. Where is the writer of the letters, and why is he there?
8. How does he meet Victor Frankenstein?
9. How does Robert feel about his guest?
10. Why is Frankenstein in the Arctic?

Chapters 1-5
1. Who is telling this part of the story?
2. How did Elizabeth come to live with the Frankensteins?
3. Who is Frankenstein's closest friend?
4. What was one of the themes of the writers who influenced Frankenstein?
5. What natural phenomena influenced Frankenstein?
6. What two major events happened to Frankenstein when he was seventeen?
7. What goal did Frankenstein decide to pursue?
8. How did Frankenstein feel when his experiment succeeded, and the creature came to life?
9. What happened to Frankenstein the day after he completed his creation?
10. Who took care of Frankenstein during his illness?

Chapters 6-9
1. What did Clerval give Frankenstein when he was better?
2. How did Frankenstein and Clerval spend the next several months?
3. What news did the letter from Frankenstein's father bring?
4. What did Frankenstein see just outside the gates of Geneva as he was returning home?
5. Who was accused of committing the murder, and why?
6. What was Frankenstein's reaction to this accusation?
7. What did Frankenstein do about his dilemma?
8. What happened to the accused person?
9. What was Frankenstein's state of mind after the trial and its conclusion?
10. Where did Frankenstein go to seek relief?

Short Answer Study Guide Questions *Frankenstein* page 2

Chapters 10-15
1. Whom did Frankenstein meet after he had ascended to the summit of Montanvert?
2. How did Frankenstein react to this meeting?
3. What did the creature want of Frankenstein?
4. How did the creature feel when he first felt life?
5. What was the reaction of the villagers the creature encountered?
6. Where did the creature take shelter?
7. What observations did the creature make about the people in the cottage?
8. What does the creature learn to do, and how does he learn this?
9. What was the elder De Lacey's reaction when the creature entered the cottage and began speaking with him?
10. What was the reaction of the De Lacey family when they saw the creature?

Chapters 16-20
1. What did the creature do at the cottage when he returned and found that the De Laceys had moved out?
2. What was the reaction of the man whose daughter was saved from drowning by the creature?
3. What discovery did the creature make when he approached another human?
4. What did the creature do to this person?
5. How did the creature feel after his deed?
6. What did the creature tell Frankenstein about the locket?
7. What did the creature ask Frankenstein to do, and why?
8. How did Frankenstein react to this request?
9. What threat did the creature make when he saw Frankenstein destroy his second creation?
10. What happened to Frankenstein when he landed his boat?

Chapter 21-24
1. Who had been the creature's most recent victim?
2. What happened at Frankenstein's trial?
3. What event occurred next in Frankenstein's life?
4. What happened on Frankenstein and Elizabeth's wedding night?
5. What happened to Frankenstein's father as a result of this latest tragedy?
6. What was the magistrate's response when Frankenstein told him the entire story of the creature?
7. What did Frankenstein do after he left the magistrate?
8. What request does Frankenstein make of Robert Walton?
9. What happened to Frankenstein at the end of the novel?
10. What happened to the creature at the end of the novel?

ANSWER KEY: SHORT ANSWER STUDY GUIDE QUESTIONS *Frankenstein*

Introduction, Preface, Letters

1. Why did Mary Shelley write Frankenstein?
    She wrote it as a response to a challenge by Lord Byron to think of a ghost story.

2. What discussions influenced the development of her idea?
    She was listening to her husband, Shelley, and Lord Byron talk about the nature of life, and the possibility of creating a creature.

3. In the preface, what does the author say she is trying to preserve?
    She is trying to "preserve the truth of the elementary principles of human nature."

4. What is the structure, or form, of the novel?
    It is an epistolary novel. This means it is written as a series of letters.

5. Who was writing the letters?
    They were written by Robert Walton.

6. To whom were the letters written?
    They were written to Walton's sister, Mrs. Margaret Saville, in England.

7. Where was the writer, and why was he there?
    He was in the Arctic, exploring unknown regions.

8. How did he meet Victor Frankenstein?
    He and the crew found Frankenstein stuck on a large piece of ice. They rescued him and brought him aboard their vessel.

9. How did Robert feel about his guest?
    He liked Frankenstein, and hoped they would become friends.

10. Why was Frankenstein in the Arctic?
    He was pursuing the creature.

Chapters 1-5

1. Who told this part of the story?
    Victor Frankenstein told his story to Robert Walton.

2. How did Elizabeth come to live with the Frankensteins?
    Caroline Frankenstein saw her with a peasant family, and offered to raise her in better circumstances.

3. Who was Frankenstein's closest friend?
    It was Henry Clerval.

4. What was one of the themes of the writers who influenced Frankenstein?
    The authors he liked wrote about raising ghosts or devils. He tried to mimic them.

5. What natural phenomena influenced Frankenstein?
    He watched a tree being hit by lightning during a storm. He became interested in the theories of electricity and galvanism.

6. What two major events happened to Frankenstein when he was seventeen?
    His mother died and he went to the university at Inglostadt to study.

7. What goal did Frankenstein decide to pursue?
    He wanted to try to renew life in a corpse, to "bestow animation upon lifeless matter."

8. How did Frankenstein feel when his experiment succeeded, and the creature came to life?
    He was horrified and disgusted.

9. What happened to Frankenstein the day after he completed his creation?
    He became ill with a fever and delirium for several months.

10. Who took care of Frankenstein during his illness?
    Henry Clerval did.

Chaters 6-9
1. What did Clerval give Frankenstein when he was better?
    He gave him a letter from Elisabeth.

2. How did Frankenstein and Clerval spend the next several months?
    Frankenstein introduced Clerval to the professors. They studied and went for walks.

3. What news did the letter from Frankenstein's father bring?
    Frankenstein's youngest brother, William, had been murdered.

4. What did Frankenstein see just outside the gates of Geneva as he was returning home?
    He saw the monster he had created.

5. Who was accused of committing the murder, and why?
   Justine, who lived with the family, was accused. She had not been with the family on the night William was murdered. Several people had seen her the next morning looking confused and frightened. A servant found the locket that Elizabeth had given to William in Justine's pocket.

6. What was Frankenstein's reaction to this accusation?
   He was sure the creature had committed the murder. He was torn between wanting to save Justine and not wanting to reveal his horrible secret to anyone. He considered himself the real murderer.

7. What did Frankenstein do about his dilemma?
   He appealed to the courts to let Justine go free, and told his family that she was innocent, but he did not tell anyone about the creature.

8. What happened to the accused person?
   She confessed under pressure from her priest. She was convicted and hanged.

9. What was Frankenstein's state of mind after the trial and its conclusion?
   He was filled with remorse for all he had done. He was also fearful that the creature would commit other crimes.

10. Where did Frankenstein go to seek relief?
    He traveled to the Alpine valley and the village of Chamounix.

<u>Chapters 10-15</u>
1. Whom did Frankenstein meet after he had ascended to the summit of Montanvert?
   He met his creature.

2. How did Frankenstein react to this meeting?
   He was full of rage and horror. He threatened to kill the creature.

3. What did the creature want of Frankenstein?
   He wanted Frankenstein to listen to the account of his life so far.

4. How did the creature feel when he first felt life?
   He felt confused because of all of the new sensations.

5. What was the reaction of the villagers the creature encountered?
   They shrieked, and threw rocks and other things at him, and drove him away from the village.

6. Where did the creature take shelter?
    He stayed in a lean-to attached to a cottage.

7. What observations did the creature make about the people in the cottage?
    He saw that they cared for each other, that the two younger people treated the older man with great respect, and that they were often sad and hungry.

8. What does the creature learn to do, and how does he learn this?
    He learns to speak, and then to read, by observing and listening to the cottagers. He found a portmanteau that had several books in it, and he read them. He then read the letters that were in the pocket of the coat he had taken from Victor Frankenstein.

9. What was the elder De Lacey's reaction when the creature entered the cottage and began speaking with him?
    The elder man was blind, and therefore could not see how hideous the creature looked. He invited the creature in and agreed to listen to his story.

10. What was the reaction of the rest of the De Lacey family when they saw the creature?
    Agatha fainted, Safie fled, and Felix hit him with a stick until he left the cottage.

Chapters 16-20
1. What did the creature do to the cottage when he returned and found that the De Laceys had moved out?
    He set fire to it in a rage.

2. What was the reaction of the man whose daughter was saved from drowning by the creature?
    He took the girl from the creature's arms, and shot the creature when he pursued the pair.

3. What discovery did the creature make when he approached another human?
    He seized a small boy, and discovered that he was William Frankenstein.

4. What did the creature do to this person?
    He strangled the boy.

5. How did the creature feel after his deed?
    He was delighted that he was able to create despair for his creator.

6. What did the creature tell Frankenstein about the locket?
    He said he found the locket on the boy, and took it. Later when he saw Justine sleeping, he put it in her pocket, intending that she should take the blame for the murder.

7. What did the creature ask Frankenstein to do, and why?
    He asked Frankenstein to create a female for him. He said that he was malicious because he was unhappy, and that if he were content he would not bother any more humans.

8. How did Frankenstein react to this request?
    At first he refused, but as the creature continued his argument, Frankenstein felt compassion for him, and finally agreed to create a female.

9. What threat did the creature make when he saw Frankenstein destroy his second creation?
    He said, "I will be with you on your wedding night."

10. What happened to Frankenstein when he landed his boat?
    He was accused of murder.

Chapters 21-24

1. Who had been the creature's most recent victim?
    It was Henry Clerval.

2. What happened at Frankenstein's trial?
    Witnesses were able to prove that he was on the Orkney Islands at the time the body of Clerval was found. He was acquitted and released.

3. What event occurred next in Frankenstein's life?
    He married Elizabeth.

4. What happened on Frankenstein and Elizabeth's wedding night?
    The creature broke into the room and killed Elizabeth.

5. What happened to Frankenstein's father as a result of this latest tragedy?
    He died of grief.

6. What was the magistrate's response when Frankenstein told him the entire story of the creature?
    The magistrate believed him, but said that he didn't think he and his men would be successful in catching the creature.

7. What did Frankenstein do after he left the magistrate?
    He decided to pursue the monster and kill him.

8. What request does Frankenstein make of Robert Walton?
    Frankenstein knows his strength is failing. He asks Robert Walton to destroy the creature if he ever has the opportunity.

9. What happened to Frankenstein?
    He died of natural causes while in the cabin on the ship.

10. What happened to the creature?
    He came into the cabin and saw the dead Frankenstein. He told Walton that he was going to travel in the far north and kill himself. We last see the creature as he floats away into the darkness on an ice raft.

MULTIPLE CHOICE STUDY QUESTIONS *Frankenstein*

<u>Introduction, Preface, Letters</u>

1. True or False: Mary Shelley wrote *Frankenstein* as a response to a challenge.
   - A. True
   - B. False

2. What discussions between Byron and Shelley influenced the development of her idea?
   - A. They were discussing Greek and Roman mythology.
   - B. They were discussing the book of Genesis.
   - C. They were discussing the nature of life.
   - D. They were discussing the recent discovery of fossil remains of early humans.

3. True or False: Mary Shelley said she was trying to preserve the truth of the elementary principles of human nature.
   - A. True
   - B. False

4. What is the structure or form of the novel?
   - A. It is historical fiction.
   - B. It is an epistolary novel.
   - C. It is a diary.
   - D. It is an autobiography.

5. Who was writing the letters?
   - A. They were written by Victor Frankenstein.
   - B. They were written by the creature.
   - C. They were written by Margaret Saville.
   - D. They were written by Robert Walton.

6. To whom were the letters written?
   - A. They were written to the writer's sister.
   - B. They were written to the world at large.
   - C. They were written to the writer's father.
   - D. They were written to the writer's confessor.

7. Where is the writer, and why is he there?
   - A. He is in the Arctic, hunting for whales.
   - B. He is in the Arctic, exploring unknown regions.
   - C. He is in Russia trapping fur.
   - D. He is in Iceland doing research on life in cold climates.

Study Guide Questions Multiple Choice Format *Frankenstein*

Introduction, Preface, Letters continued

8. True or False: Frankenstein was one of the sailors.
    A. True
    B. False

9. How does Robert feel about Frankenstein?
    A. He thinks Frankenstein is crazy, but likable.
    B. He doesn't like Frankenstein. He thinks he is a liar.
    C. He doesn't trust Frankenstein.
    D. He likes Frankenstein, and hopes they will become friends.

10. True or False: Frankenstein is in the Arctic to escape from the creature.
    A. True
    B. False

Study Guide Questions Multiple Choice Format *Frankenstein*

<u>Chapters 1-5</u>
1. True or False: In this part of the story, Frankenstein is telling his story to Robert Walton.
    A. True
    B. False

2. How did Elizabeth come to live with the Frankensteins?
    A. She was left on their doorstep by her poor mother.
    B. Victor's mother asked the peasants she lived with for permission to raise her.
    C. She was adopted from an orphanage.
    D. She was the daughter of Alphonse Frankenstein's dead friend.

3. True or False: Victor Frankenstein and Henry Clerval had been friends since childhood.
    A. True
    B. False

4. True or False: The authors Frankenstein enjoyed talked about the life of the soul in heaven.
    A. True
    B. False

5. What natural phenomena influenced Frankenstein?
    A. It was an avalanche.
    B. It was a waterfall.
    C. It was lightning.
    D. It was a tornado.

6. What two major events happened to Frankenstein when he was seventeen?
    A. His youngest brother was born and he fell in love.
    B. He received his inheritance and traveled abroad.
    C. His mother died and he went to the university at Inglostadt to study.
    D. He got his first job and moved to his own apartment.

7. True or False: Frankenstein wanted to try to create life in a test tube.
    A. True
    B. False

Study Guide Questions Multiple Choice Format *Frankenstein*
Chapters 1-5 continued

8. How did Frankenstein feel when his experiment succeeded, and the creature came to life?
    A. He was thrilled.
    B. He was horrified and disgusted.
    C. He was excited, but scared.
    D. He felt omnipotent.

9. What type of illness afflicted Frankenstein the day after he completed his creation?
    A. He went crazy, acting like a "mad scientist."
    B. He became manic and started thinking of ways to improve his experiment.
    C. He became depressed and tried to commit suicide.
    D. He became ill with a fever and delirium for several months.

10. Who took care of Frankenstein during his illness?
    A. Henry Clerval did.
    B. Elizabeth did.
    C. His father did.
    D. He hired a nurse.

Study Guide Questions Multiple Choice Format *Frankenstein*

<u>Chapters 6-9</u>

1. From whom was the letter that Clerval gave Frankenstein when he had recovered?
    A. It was from the creature.
    B. It was from Professor Krempe.
    C. It was from Elizabeth.
    D. It was from his brother Ernest.

2. True or False: Frankenstein and Clerval spent the next few months preparing a new experiment
    A. True
    B. False

3. Frankenstein received news that his brother Ernest had been murdered.
    A. True
    B. False

4. Where did Frankenstein see the creature?
    A. The creature was hiding behind a tree at the funeral.
    B. The creature intercepted him on the road on his way home.
    C. He saw the creature on the streets of Ingolstadt.
    D. Frankenstein saw him just outside the gates of Geneva as he was returning home.

5. Who was accused of committing the murder?
    A. Justine, who lived with the family, was accused of committing the murder.
    B. Jean-Claude, one of the servants, was accused of committing the murder.
    C. Frankenstein's brother was accused of committing the murder.
    D. Jason, one of the boy's friends, was accused of committing the murder.

6. True or False: Frankenstein was torn between wanting to save the accused and not wanting to reveal his horrible secret to anyone.
    A. True
    B. False

7. True or False: Frankenstein told the judges the true story, but they didn't believe him.
    A. True
    B. False

Study Guide Questions Multiple Choice Format *Frankenstein*

Chapters 6-9 continued

8. What happened to the accused person?
    A. The accused person was found innocent and released.
    B. The accused person confessed under pressure, and was convicted and hanged.
    C. The accused person committed suicide in prison.
    D. Frankenstein helped the accused person escape from prison and flee the country.

9. What was Frankenstein's state of mind after the trial and its conclusion?
    A. He was relieved that it was over.
    B. He was sure the creature was finished with his evil deeds.
    C. He was filled with remorse for all he had done.
    D. He was inspired to create a better creature.

10. Where did Frankenstein go to seek relief?
    A. He went to a monastery in France.
    B. He went back to the university.
    C. he went to a hospital in Geneva.
    D. He traveled to the Apine valley and the village of Chamounix.

Study Guide Questions Multiple Choice Format *Frankenstein*

Chapters 10-15

1. Where did Frankenstein meet his creature?
	A. They met in Inglostadt.
	B. They met in Geneva.
	C. They met at the summit of Montanvert.
	D. They met on the bridge of Pelissier.

2. True or False: Frankenstein was delighted to finally meet the creature.
	A. True
	B. False

3. What did the creature want of Frankenstein?
	A. He wanted money and food.
	B. He wanted a place to live.
	C. He wanted to go back to the university and study with Frankenstein.
	D. He wanted Frankenstein to listen to the account of his life so far.

4. Tue or False: At first, the creature felt confused because of all of the new sensations of life.
	A. True
	B. False

5. True or False: The villagers the creature encountered were awed and worshiped the creature as a god.
	A. True
	B. False

6. Where did the creature take shelter?
	A. He built a log cabin in the woods.
	B. He slept out in the open, because he didn't need protection from the elements.
	C. He stayed in a lean-to attached to a cottage.
	D. He found a cave in the mountains and lived there.

7. Which of the following was not an observation made by the creature about the De Laceys'?
	A. They cared for each other.
	B. The two younger people treated the older man with great respect.
	C. They were often hungry.
	D. They were very happy in spite of their situation.

Study Guide Questions Multiple Choice Format *Frankenstein*

Chapters 10-15 continued

8. How did the creature learn to speak and to read?
    A. He observed and listened to the cottagers.
    B. Frankenstein had programmed his brain to know how immediately.
    C. He sat outside the local school house and listened.
    D. A young child befriended him and taught him.

9. True or False: The elder De Lacey was blind, and therefore could not see how hideous the creature looked. He invited the creature in and agreed to listen to his story.
    A. True
    B. False

10. What was the reaction of the rest of the De Lacey family when they saw the creature?
    A. Agatha welcomed him, but Safie and Felix threw stones at him.
    B. Agatha fainted, Safie fled, and Felix hit him with a stick until he left the cottage.
    C. Safie thought her father had sent him to take her away. Felix shot at him.
    D. The father told them all to run away, then he tried to persuade the creature to leave.

Study Guide Questions Multiple Choice Format *Frankenstein*

Chapters 16-20

1. When the creature found that the De Laceys had moved out of the cottage, he moved in.
    A. True
    B. False

2. Whom did the creature save?
    A. He saved a woman who had become separated from her friends.
    B. He saved a mountain climber who had fallen.
    C. He saved a shepherd and his flock from being attacked by wolves.
    D. He saved a girl from drowning.

3. Who was the small boy seized by the creature?
    A. Alphonse Frankenstein
    B. William Frankenstein
    C. Ernest Frankenstein
    D. Henry Clerval

4. What did the creature do to the boy?
    A. He drowned the boy.
    B. He threw the boy off a cliff.
    C. He strangled the boy.
    D. He beat the boy to death.

5. True or False: The creature was delighted that he was able to create despair for his creator.
    A. True
    B. False

6. Why did the creature put the locket in Justine's pocket?
    A. He wanted to return it to the Frankenstein family as a warning.
    B. He intended that she should take the blame for the murder.
    C. He didn't know what it was, and he didn't need it.
    D. He wanted to give her a gift, hoping she would like him.

7. True or False: The creature asked Frankenstein to teach him how to create another life.
    A. True
    B. False

Study Guide Questions Multiple Choice Format *Frankenstein*

Chapters 16-20 continued

8. True or False: At first Frankenstein refused, but as the creature continued his argument, Frankenstein felt compassion for him, and finally agreed to the creature's request.
    A. True
    B. False

9. What threat did the creature make when Frankenstein backed out on their agreement?
    A. He said, "All of mankind is now cursed."
    B. He said, "I will pursue you to the ends of the earth and the end of your life."
    C. He said, "I will be with you on your wedding night."
    D. He said, "Alas, I am doomed to a wretched life on this earth!"

10. What happened to Frankenstein when he landed his boat?
    A. He fainted from exhaustion.
    B. The creature found him and beat him.
    C. He got drunk to forget what he had done.
    D. He was accused of murder.

Study Guide Questions Multiple Choice Format *Frankenstein*

Chapters 21-24

1. Who had been the creature's most recent victim?
    A. It was the wife of the local doctor.
    B. It was Alphonse Frankenstein.
    C. It was one of Frankenstein's cousins who lived in the village.
    D. It was Henry Clerval.

2. True or False: At the trial, Frankenstein was found innocent by reason of insanity.
    A. True
    B. False

3. What event occurred next in Frankenstein's life?
    A. He went to England to study.
    B. He went to a mental institution to try and recover.
    C. He married Elizabeth.
    D. He went back to the university.

4. What happened on Frankenstein and Elizabeth's wedding night?
    A. The Creature kidnaped Elizabeth.
    B. The creature attacked Victor, but Frankenstein managed to escape.
    C. The creature attacked both of them, but only killed Elizabeth.
    D. The creature broke into the room and killed Elizabeth.

5. True or False: Frankenstein's father went insane with grief and had to be institutionalized.
    A. True
    B. False

6. True or False: The magistrate believed Frankenstein's story, but said that he didn't think he and his men would be successful in catching the creature.
    A. True
    B. False

7. What did Frankenstein do after he left the magistrate?
    A. He went on a sea voyage to escape from the creature.
    B. He went to the professors at the university for help.
    C. He decided to pursue the creature and kill him.
    D. He hired a group of men to hunt and kill the creature.

Study Guide Questions Multiple Choice Format *Frankenstein*

Chapters 21-24 continued

8. What request did Frankenstein make of Robert Walton?
    A. He asked Walton to destroy the creature if he ever had the opportunity.
    B. He asked Walton to get him to a doctor as soon as possible..
    C. He asked Walton to tell his story so that others will not make the same mistake.
    D. He asked Walton to reason with the creature and get him to surrender.

9. True or False: The creature strangled Victor Frankenstein.
    A. True
    B. False

10. What happened to the creature?
    A. He broke his neck as he tried to jump from the ship.
    B. He laughed and said he would continue to seek vengeance on humanity.
    C. He floated away into the darkness on an ice raft.
    D. Walton shot and killed him.

ANSWER KEY - MULTIPLE CHOICE STUDY/QUIZ QUESTIONS
Frankenstein

Introduction, Preface, Letters
1. A True
2. C
3. A True
4. B
5. D
6. A
7. B
8. B False
9. D
10. B False

Chapter 1-5
1. A True
2. B
3. A True
4. B False
5. C
6. C
7. B False
8. B
9. D
10. A

Chapters 6-9
1. C
2. B False
3. B False
4. D
5. A
6. A True
7. B False
8. B
9. C
10. D

Chapters 10-15
1. C
2. B False
3. D
4. A True
5. B
6. C
7. D
8. A
9. A True
10. B

Chapters 16-20
1. B False
2. D
3. B
4. C
5. A True
6. B
7. B False
8. A True
9. C
10. D

Chapters 21-24
1. D
2. B False
3. C
4. D
5. B False
6. A True
7. C
8. A
9. B False
10. C

PREREADING VOCABULARY WORKSHEETS

Vocabulary - *Frankenstein*

Introduction, Preface, Letters
Part I: Using Prior Knowledge and Contextual Clues
Below are the sentences in which the vocabulary words appear in the text. Read the sentence. Use any clues you can find in the sentence combined with your prior knowledge, and write what you think the underlined words mean in the space provided.

1. "...how I, then a young girl, came to think of, and to *dilate* upon, so very hideous an idea?"

2. His success would terrify the artist; he would rush away from his *odious* handiwork, horror-stricken.

3. And now, once again, I bid my hideous *progeny* go forth and prosper.

4. It was commenced partly as a source of amusement and partly as an *expedient* for exercising any untried resources of mind.

5. I have no one near me, gentle yet courageous, possessed of a cultivated as well as of a *capacious* mind, whose tastes are like my own, to approve or amend my plans.

6. I am too *ardent* in execution, and too impatient of difficulties.

7. His limbs were nearly frozen, and his body dreadfully *emaciated* by fatigue and suffering.

8. I never saw a man in so *wretched* a condition.

9. Such words, you may imagine, strongly excited my curiosity; but the *paroxysm* of grief that had seized the stranger overcame his weakened powers....

10. Strange and *harrowing* must be his story.

Vocabulary - *Frankenstein*

Introduction, Preface, Letters continued

Part II: Determining the Meaning   Match the vocabulary words to their dictionary definitions.

___ 1. dilate   A. spasm, convulsion

___ 2. odious   B. children, offspring

___ 3. progeny   C. thin, wasted

___ 4. expedient   D. expand

___ 5. capacious   E. distressing, agonizing

___ 6. ardent   F. passionate, enthusiastic

___ 7. emaciated   G. suitable, practical

___ 8. wretched   H. hateful

___ 9. paroxysm   I. miserable

___10. harrowing   J. spacious, roomy

Vocabulary - *Frankenstein* Chapter 1 - 5

Part I: Using Prior Knowledge and Contextual Clues
Below are the sentences in which the vocabulary words appear in the text. Read the sentence. Use any clues you can find in the sentence combined with your prior knowledge, and write what you think the underlined words mean in the space provided.

1. This man, whose name was Beaufort, was of a proud and unbending disposition and could not bear to live in poverty and *oblivion* in the same country where he had formerly been distinguished for his rank and magnificence.

2. . . . his grief only became more deep and *rankling* when he had leisure for reflection, and at length it took so fast hold of his mind that at the end of three months he lay on a bed of sickness, incapable of an exertion.

3. During one of their walks a poor cot in the foldings of a vale attracted their notice as being singularly disconsolate, while the number of half-clothed children gathered about it spoke of *penury* in it worst shape.

4. By one of those *caprices* of the mind which we are perhaps most subject to in early youth, I at once gave up my former occupations, set down natural history and all its progeny as a deformed and abortive creation, and entertained the greatest disdain for a would-be science which could never even step within the threshold of real knowledge.

5. He then took a *cursory* view of the present state of the science and explained many of its elementary terms.

6. On the third day my mother sickened; her fever was accompanied by the most alarming symptons, and the looks of her medical attendants *prognosticated* the worst.

7. She died calmly, and her *countenance* expressed affection even in death.

8. He was respected by all who knew him for his integrity and *indefatigable* attention to public business.

9. . . . and I found even in M. Krempe a great deal of sound sense and real information, combined, it is true, with a repulsive *physiognomy* and manners, but not on that account the less valuable.

10. But this discovery was so great and overwhelming that all the steps by which I had been progressively let to it were *obliterated*, and I beheld only the result.

Part II. Determining the Meaning   Match the vocabulary words to their dictionary definitions.

____1. oblivion   A. irritating

____2. rankling   B. hastily done

____3. penury   C. tireless

____4. caprice   D. destroying completely

____5. cursory   E. face

____6. prognosticated   F. facial features with regard to revealing character

____7. countenance   G. whim

____8. indefatigable   H. predicted

____9. physiognomy   I. extreme poverty

____10. obliterated   J. State of being forgotten

Vocabulary - *Frankenstein* Chapters 1-5 continued

The meanings of the following words are necessary to understanding the story, but will not be tested.

I am by birth a *Genevese*, and my family is one of the most distinguished of that republic. My ancestors had been for may years *counsellors* and *syndics*....
Genevese–a native or inhabitant of Geneva, Switzerland
counsellors–an attorney or trial lawyer
syndics–civil magistrates

In this house I chanced to find a volume of the works of *Cornelius Agrippa*.
Cornelius Agrippa (1486-1535) was as a young man interested in alchemy, astrology, and natural magic.

Under the guidance of my new preceptors, I entered with the greatest diligence into the search of the *philosopher's stone* and the *elixir of life*....
The alchemists thought that the philosopher's stone would give its owner the power to change metals into gold. The elixir of life was thought to be able to give eternal life to the one who could distill it.

Vocabulary - *Frankenstein* Chapters 6-9

Part I: Using Prior Knowledge and Contextual Clues

Below are the sentences in which the vocabulary words appear in the text. Read the sentence. Use any clues you can find in the sentence combined with your prior knowledge, and write what you think the underlined words mean in the space provided.

1. He looks upon study as an odious *fetter*; his time is spent in the open air, climbing the hills or rowing on the lake.

2. The blue lake, the snow-clad mountains, they never change; and I think our placid home, and our contented hears are regulated by the same *immutable* laws.

3. The poor woman was very *vacillating* in her repentance.

4. We passed a fortnight in these perambulations: my health and spirits had long been restored, and they gained additional strength from the *salubrious* air I breathed, the natural incidents of our progress, and the conversation of my friend.

5. Alas! I had turned loose into the world a depraved wretch, whose delight was in *carnage* and misery; had he not murdered my bother?

6. Justine also was a girl of merit, and possessed qualities which promised to render her life happy: now all was to be obliterated in an *ignominious* grave; and I the cause!

7. ...but fear, and hatred of the crime of which they supposed her guilty, rendered them *timorous*, and unwilling to come forward.

8. He threatened excommunication and hell fire in my last moments, if I continued *obdurate.*

9. Dear lady, I had none to support me; all looked on me as a wretch doomed to ignominy and *perdition*.

10. ...happy beyond his hopes, if this *inexorable* fate be satisfied, and if the destruction pause before the peace of the grave have succeeded to your sad torments.

Vocabulary - *Frankenstein* Chapters 6-9 continued

Part II: Determining the Meaning   Match the vocabulary words to their dictionary definitions.

___ 1. fetter   A. destruction of life

___ 2. immutable   B. relentless, unyielding

___ 3. vacillating   C. shackle

___ 4. salubrious   D. disgraceful

___ 5. carnage   E. damnation, complete ruin

___ 6. ignominious   F. unchanging

___ 7. timorous   G. fearful

___ 8. obdurate   H. fluctuating, wavering

___ 9. perdition   I. stubborn

___10. inexorable   J. healthful

Vocabulary - *Frankenstein* Chapters 10-15

Part I: Using Prior Knowledge and Contextual Clues

   Below are the sentences in which the vocabulary words appear in the text. Read the sentence. Use any clues you can find in the sentence combined with your prior knowledge, and write what you think the underlined words mean in the space provided.

1. The ascent is *precipitous*, but the path is cut into continual and short windings, which enable you to surmount the perpendicularity of the mountain.

2. Listen to my tale: when you have heard that, abandon or *commiserate* me, as you shall judge that I deserve.

3. I *slaked* my thirst at the brook; and the lying down, was overcome by sleep.

4. He turned on hearing a noise, and perceiving me, shrieked loudly, and quitting the hut, ran across the fields with a speed of which his *debilitated* form hardly appeared capable.

5. Here then I retreated, and lay down happy to have found a shelter, however miserable, from the *inclemency* of the season, and still more from the barbarity of man.

6.& 7. I had first, however, provided for my *sustenance* for the day, by a loaf of coarse bread, which I *purloined*, and a cup with which I could drink...

8. The silver hair and *benevolent* countenance of the aged cottager won my reverence, while the gentle manner of the girl enticed my love.

9. The mild *exhortations* of the old man, and the lively conversation of the loved Felix were not for me.

10. A residence in Turkey was *abhorrent* to her; her religion and her feelings were alike adverse to it.

Vocabulary - *Frankenstein* Chapters 10-15 continued

Part II: Determining the Meaning   Match the vocabulary words to their dictionary definitions.

___ 1. precipitous   A. steep

___ 2. commiserate   B. quenched

___ 3. slaked   C. storminess

___ 4. debilitated   D. stolen

___ 5. inclemency   E. urgings

___ 6. sustenance   F. detested, hated

___ 7. purloined   G. generous

___ 8. benevolent   H. means of food or nourishment

___ 9. exhortations   I. weakened

___10. abhorrent   J. feel or express sympathy for

Vocabulary - *Frankenstein* Chapters 16-20

Part I: Using Prior Knowledge and Contextual Clues

   Below are the sentences in which the vocabulary words appear in the text. Read the sentence. Use any clues you can find in the sentence combined with your prior knowledge, and write what you think the underlined words mean in the space provided.

1. Why, in that instant, did I not extinguish the spark of existence which you had so *wantonly* bestowed?

2. My sufferings were *augmented* also by the oppressive sense of the injustice and ingratitude of their affliction.

3. The child still struggled, and loaded me with *epithets* which carried despair to my heart: I grasped his throat to silence him, and in a moment he lay dead at my feet.

4. Thanks to the lessons of Felix and the *sanguinary* laws of man, I had learned now to work mischief.

5. This passion is *detrimental* to me; for you do not reflect that you are the cause of its excess.

6. After some days spent in listless *indolence*, during which I traversed many leagues, I arrived at Strasbourg, where I waited for two days for Clerval.

7. I visited Edinburgh with *languid* eyes and mind; and yet that city might have interested the most unfortunate being.

8. I had before been moved by the *sophisms* of the being I had created; I had been struck senseless by his fiendish threats...

9. I was alone; none were near me to dissipate the gloom, and relieve me from the sickening oppression of the most terrible *reveries.*

10. Little did I then expect the *calamity* that was in a few moments to overwhelm me, and extinguish in horror and despair all fear of ignominy or death.

Vocabulary - *Frankenstein* Chapters 16-20 continued

Part II: Determining the Meaning Match the vocabulary words to their dictionary definitions.

___ 1. wantonly   A. weary, listless

___ 2. augmented   B. abusive words or phrases

___ 3. epithets   C. immorally, cruelly

___ 4. sanguinary   D. daydreams

___ 5. detrimental   E. bloody

___ 6. indolence   F. laziness

___ 7. languid   G. disaster

___ 8. sophisms   H. believable but misleading arguments

___ 9. reveries   I. increased

___ 10. calamity   J. harmful, damaging

Vocabulary - *Frankenstein* Chapters 21-24

Part I: Using Prior Knowledge and Contextual Clues

Below are the sentences in which the vocabulary words appear in the text. Read the sentence. Use any clues you can find in the sentence combined with your prior knowledge, and write what you think the underlined words mean.

1. Mr. Kirwin, on hearing this evidence, desired that I should be taken into the room where the body lay for *internment*, that it might be observed what effect the sight of it would produce upon me.

2. As Mr. Kirwin said this, notwithstanding the agitation I endured on this *retrospect* of my sufferings, I also felt considerable surprise at the knowledge he seemed to possess concerning me

3. I should have thought, young man, that the presence of your father would have been welcome, instead of inspiring such violent *repugnance.*

4. By the utmost self-violence, I curbed the *imperious* voice of wretchedness, which sometimes desired to declare itself to the whole world.

5. In this manner many *appalling* hours passed; several of my dogs died; and I myself was about to sink under the accumulation of distress when I saw your vessel...

6. "Since you have preserved my narration," said he, "I would not that a mutilated one should go down to *posterity*."

7. I am interrupted. What do these sounds *portend* ?

8. If you had listened to the voices of conscience and heeded the sting of remorse, before you had urged your *diabolical* vengeance to this extremity, Frankenstein would yet have lived.

9. If thou were yet alive, and yet cherished a desire of revenge against me, it would be better *satiated* in my life than in my destruction.

10. The light of that *conflagration* will fade away; my ashes will be swept into the sea by the winds.

Vocabulary - *Frankenstein* Chapters 21-24 Continued

Part II: Determining the Meaning Match the vocabulary words to their dictionary definitions.

___ 1. interment   A. domineering

___ 2. retrospect   B. shocking, dismaying

___ 3. repugnance   C. burial

___ 4. imperious   D. fully satisfied

___ 5. appalling   E. a great fire

___ 6. posterity   F. future generations

___ 7. portend   G. looking

___ 8. diabolical   H. devilish

___ 9. satiated   I. loathing

___ 10. conflagration   J. predict

ANSWER KEY - VOCABULARY *Frankenstein*

Introduction
1. D
2. H
3. B
4. G
5. J
6. F
7. C
8. I
9. A
10. E

Chapters 1-5
1. J
2. A
3. I
4. G
5. B
6. H
7. E
8. C
9. F
10. D

Chapters 6-9
1. C
2. F
3. H
4. J
5. A
6. D
7. G
8. I
9. E
10. B

Chapters 10-15
1. A
2. J
3. B
4. I
5. C
6. H
7. D
8. G
9. E
10. F

Chapters 16-20
1. C
2. I
3. B
4. E
5. J
6. F
7. A
8. H
9. D
10. G

Chapters 21-24
1. C
2. G
3. I
4. A
5. B
6. F
7. J
8. H
9. D
10. E

DAILY LESSONS

LESSON ONE

Objectives
    1. To introduce the *Frankenstein* unit
    2. To relate students' prior knowledge to the new material
    3. To distribute books and other related materials
    4. To introduce the characteristics of the gothic novel
    5. To do the prereading work for the Introduction, Preface, and Letters

Activity 1

    Play some eerie "mood music" related to *Frankenstein* or to horror stories in general. Display a picture or a poster of the Frankenstein creature. Most of the students will know something about the story. Do a group KWL sheet with student (form included). Put any information the students know in the K column (What I Know). Ask students what they want to find out and put that information in the W column (What I Want To Find Out). keep the sheet and refer back to it after reading the novel to complete the L column (What I Learned).

Activity 2

    Distribute the materials students will use in this unit. Explain in detail how students are to use these materials.

    Study Guides Students should preview the study guide questions before each reading assignment to get a feeling for what events and ideas are important in that section. After reading the section, students will (as a class or individually) answer the questions to review the important events and ideas from that section of the book. Students should keep the study guides as study materials for the unit test.

    Vocabulary Prior to reading a reading assignment, students will do vocabulary work related to the section of the book they are about to read. Following the completion of the reading of the book, there will be a vocabulary review of all the words used in the vocabulary assignments. Students should keep their vocabulary work as study materials for the unit test.

    Reading Assignment Sheet You need to fill in the reading assignment sheet to let students know when their reading has to be completed. You can either write the assignment sheet on a side blackboard or bulletin board and leave it there for students to see each day, or you can "ditto" copies for each student to have. In either case, you should advise students to become very familiar with the reading assignments so they know what is expected of them.

    Extra Activities Center The Unit Resources of this unit contains suggestions for a library of related books and articles in your classroom as well as crossword and word search puzzles. Make an extra activities center in your room where you will keep these materials for students to use. (Bring the books and articles in from the library and keep several copies of the puzzles on hand.) Explain to students that these materials are available for students to use when they finish reading assignments or other class work early.

       <u>Nonfiction Assignment Sheet</u> Explain to students that they each are to read at least one non-fiction piece from the in-class library at some time during the unit. Students will fill out a nonfiction assignment sheet after completing the reading to help you evaluate their reading experiences and to help the students think about and evaluate their own reading experiences.

       <u>Books</u> Each school has its own rules and regulations regarding student use of school books. Advise students of the procedures that are normal for your school.

Activity #3

       Introduce the characteristics of the gothic horror story. The term "gothic" refers to an emphasis on the grotesque (such as the creature's physical characteristics), the mysterious (such as Frankenstein's never explaining how he gave life to his creature or how they could conduct a pursuit all the way to the Arctic), a desolate environment (the Arctic), horrible occurrences (the many murders), the ghostly (the creature's appearing out of nowhere, fog rainstorms), and fear. Remind students to keep these elements in mind as they are reading.

Activity #4

       Show students how to preview the study questions and do the vocabulary work for the Introduction Preface, and Letters of *Frankenstein*. If students do not finish this assignment in class, they should complete it prior to the next class meeting.

LESSON TWO

Objectives
    1. To read the Introduction, Preface, and Letters
    2. To review the main ideas and events from the Introduction, Preface, and Letters
    3. To introduce the Nonfiction Assignment

Activity 1

    You may want to read the Introduction and Preface aloud to the students to set the mood for the novel. Invite willing students to read the letters aloud to the rest of the class.

Activity 2

    There are only a few study guide questions for this section. Give the students time to answer them and then discuss the answers in detail. Write the answers on the board or overhead projector so students can have the correct answers for study purposes. Encourage students to take notes. If the students own their books, encourage tem to use high lighter pens to mark important passages and the answers to the study questions.

    Note: It is a good practice in public speaking and leadership skills for individual students to take charge of leading the discussions of the study questions. Perhaps a different student could goo in front of the class and lead the discussion each day that the study questions are discussed during this unit. Of course, the teacher should guide the discussion when appropriate and be sure to fill in any gaps the students leave.

Activity 3

    Distribute copies of the Nonfiction Assignment sheet and discuss it with the class. Give them the due date for the assignment (Lesson 17).

NONFICTION READING ASSIGNMENT SHEET - *Frankenstein*
(To be completed after reading the required nonfiction article)

Name _____ Date _____

Title of Nonfiction Read _____

Written By _____ Publication Date _____

I. Factual Summary: Write a short summary of the piece you read.

II. Vocabulary
 1. With which vocabulary words in the piece did you encounter some degree of difficulty?

 2. How did you resolve your lack of understanding with these words?

III. Interpretation: What was the main point the author wanted you to get from reading his work?

IV. Criticism
 1. With which points of the piece did you agree or find easy to accept? Why?

 2. With which points of the piece did you disagree or find difficult to believe? Why?

V. Personal Response: What do you think about this piece? OR How does this piece influence your ideas?

KWL

Directions: Before reading, think about what you already know about Mary Shelley and/or *Frankenstein*. Write the information in the **K** column. Think about what you would like to find out from reading the book. Write your questions in the **W** column. After you have read the book, use the **L** column to write the answers to your questions from the W column, and anything else you remember from the book.

K What I Know	**W** What I Want to Find Out	**L** What I Learned

LESSON THREE

Objectives

    1. To do the prereading and vocabulary work for chapters 1-5
    2. To read chapters 1-5
    3. To give students practice reading orally
    4. To evaluate students' oral reading

Activity #1

    Give students about fifteen minutes to preview the study questions for chapters 1-5 ad do the related vocabulary work.

Activity #2

    Have students read chapters 1-5 of *Frankenstein* out loud in class. You probably know the best way to get readers with your class; pick students at random, ask for volunteers, or use whatever method works best for your group. If you have not yet completed an oral reading evaluation for your students for this marking period, this would be a good opportunity to do so. A form is included for your convenience. If students do not complete reading chapters 1-5 in class, they should do so prior to the next class meeting.

LESSON FOUR

Objectives

    1. To review the main events and ideas from chapters 1-5
    2. To familiarize students with vocabulary from chapters6-9
    3. To preview study questions for chapters 6-9
    4. To read chapters 6-9

Activity #1

    Use the multiple choice format of the study guide questions for chapters1-5 as a quiz to check that students have done the required reading and to review the main ideas of chapters 1-5. Exchange papers for checking. Discuss answers and make sure students take notes for studying purposes.

Activity #2

    Give students about fifteen minutes to preview the study questions for chapters 6-9 and to do the related vocabulary

Activity #3

    Have students read chapters 6-9 for the rest of the period. If you have not completed the oral reading evaluations, do so now. If the evaluations have been completed, you may want the students to read silently. If students do not complete the reading assignment in class, they should do so prior to your next class meeting.

ORAL READING EVALUATION - *Frankenstein*

Name _____ Class____ Date _____

SKILL	EXCELLENT	GOOD	AVERAGE	FAIR	POOR
Fluency	5	4	3	2	1
Clarity	5	4	3	2	1
Audibility	5	4	3	2	1
Pronunciation	5	4	3	2	1
_____	5	4	3	2	1
_____	5	4	3	2	1

Total _____   Grade _____

Comments:

LESSON FIVE

Objectives
1. To give students the opportunity to practice writing directions for performing a task
2. To give the teacher the opportunity to evaluate each student's writing skills

Activity 1

Distribute Writing Assignment 1 and discuss the directions in detail. Allow the remaining class time for students to work on the assignment. Give students an additional two or three days to complete the assignment if necessary.

Activity 2

Distribute copies of the Writing Evaluation Form. Explain to students that during Lesson Nine you will be holding individual writing conferences about this writing assignment. Make sure they are familiar with the criteria on the Writing Evaluation Form.

Follow-Up: After you have graded the assignments, have a writing conference with each student. After the writing conference, allow students to revise their papers using your suggestions to complete the revision. We suggest grading the revisions on an A-C-E scale (all revisions done, some revisions made, few or no revisions made). This will speed your grading time and still give some credit for the students' efforts.

LESSON SIX

Objectives
1. To review the main ideas of chapters 6-9
2. To do the prereading vocabulary work and study questions for chapters 10-15
3. To read chapters 10-15 silently

Activity #1

Ask students to get out their books and some paper (not their study guides). Tell students to write down ten questions and answers which cover the main events and ideas in chapters 6-9. Discuss the students' questions and answers orally, making a list on the board of the questions with brief responses. Put a star next to students' questions and answers that are essentially the same as the study guide questions. Be sure that all the study guide questions are represented.

Activity #2

Have students pair up and do the prereading and vocabulary work together for chapters 10-15.

Activity #3

Give students the remainder of the class time to begin silently reading chapters 10-15. Remind them that the reading must be completed prior to your next class meeting.

WRITING ASSIGNMENT 1 - *Frankenstein*

PROMPT

Victor Frankenstein was a scientist. During his experiment to discover when life began, and to "bestow animation upon lifeless matter" he kept detailed records of his procedures. Presumably, if someone wanted to duplicate his experiment, they could do so from Frankenstein's notes.

your assignment is to write directions for making or doing something. It should be easy enough for your classmates or teachers to do in two hours or less.

PREWRITING

The first thing you need to do is decide what yo want to write directions for. Do you want to explain how to make your favorite sandwich? Perhaps you want to give directions for changing the tire on a car or bike. You may choose any topic as long as the process you describe has at least four steps.

Next, go through the entire process yourself. Keep a notebook with you and record your steps as you do them. These notes need to be very precise. Include directional words (up, down, next to, etc.) if necessary. Make sure to number the steps. Make a supply list and include everything that you used.

If you can work with a friend, you can go through the process and have the friend take notes. Another approach is to audio or video tape yourself as you perform the procedure and then go back and transcribe what you see to notes.

DRAFTING

First, write a paragraph in which you introduce the product or process. Tell what it is and why you chose it. Describe the product in enough detail that the reader will be able to visualize it. Give an estimate of how long it should take the reader to follow your directions and complete the procedure.

In the body of your paper, list all the supplies that are needed. Then list the directions in sequential order. You may find it easier to use a list format here instead of a paragraph. In either case, you must number the steps.

Finally, write a concluding paragraph that tells again what the finished product should look like or what the results of the completed procedure are. You may want to remind your readers to go back and double-check their work.

PROMPT

When you finish the rough draft of your paper, ask another student to read it. After reading your rough draft, he/she should tell you what he/she liked best about your work, which parts were difficult to understand, and ways in which your work could be improved. Reread your paper considering your critic's comments and make the corrections you think are necessary.

PROOFREADING

Do a final proofreading of your paper, double-checking your grammar, spelling, organization, and the clarity of your ideas.

WRITING EVALUATION FORM - *Frankenstein*

Name _____ Date _____

Writing Assignment #1 for the *Frankenstein* unit   Grade _____

Circle One For Each Item:

Introduction	excellent	good	fair	poor
Body Paragraphs	excellent	good	fair	poor
Conclusion	excellent	good	fair	poor
Grammar:	excellent	good	fair	poor (errors noted)
Spelling:	excellent	good	fair	poor (errors noted)
Punctuation:	excellent	good	fair	poor (errors noted)
Legibility:	excellent	good	fair	poor

Strengths:

Weaknesses:

Comments/Suggestions:

LESSON SEVEN

Objectives

    1. To review the main ideas and events from chapters 10-15
    2. To preview the study questions and vocabulary for chapters 16-20
    3. To read chapters 16-20

Activity 1

    Review the study guide questions and answers for chapters 10-15.

Activity 2

    Give students about 15 minutes to complete the prereading and vocabulary work for chapters 16-20.

Activity 3

    Depending on the needs of your group, have the students read chapters 16-20 orally or silently. Remind them that any reading not completed in class must be finished before the next class meeting.

LESSON EIGHT

Objectives

    1. To check to see that students have done the required reading
    2. To introduce Writing Assignment 2

Activity 1

    Give students a quiz on chapters 16-20. Use either the short answer or multiple choice form of the study guide questions as a quiz so that in discussing the answers to the quiz you also answer the study questions. Collect papers for grading.

Activity 2

    Distribute Writing Assignment 2. Discuss the directions in detail and give students ample time to complete the assignment.

LESSON NINE

Objectives

    1. To have students revise their first writing assignment papers
    2. To work on other assignments independently

Activity

    Call students to your desk or some other private area to discuss their papers from Writing Assignment 1. Use the completed Writing Evaluation Form as a basis for your critique. Students should use this period (when they are not conferencing with you) to work on their Nonfiction assignment or to review the study guide questions they have covered so far.

WRITING ASSIGNMENT 2 - *Frankenstein*

PROMPT

Justine Moritz was accused of murdering William Frankenstein. The sole evidence was the locket that had been placed in her pocket by the creature. Although she had several character witnesses and Victor interceded in her behalf, she was still found guilty.

In this writing assignment, Justine Moritz is entitled to a new trial by jury before she is convicted and sentenced. You are to act either as the defense (for Justine) or the prosecution (against Justine). Your assignment is to write a closing argument to the jury. (A closing argument is a lawyer's final summary of his/her case and the best efforts at persuading the jury to his/her side.)

PREWRITING

To begin, decide which side you want to take–the defense or the prosecution. On a piece of paper, jot down the main points, the facts which will support your case. Decide which points are your strongest and which of the arguments you will make are weaker. Organize your points from weakest to strongest and jot down anything you can think of which will support or explain your points.

DRAFTING

Begin with an introductory paragraph in which you introduce the jury to your side of the case. Follow that with one paragraph for each of the main points you have to support your case. Fill in each paragraph with examples and facts which support your main point. Then, write a paragraph in which you make your final closing statements.

PROMPT

When you finish the rough draft of your paper, ask a student who sits near you to read it. After reading your rough draft, he/she should tell you what he/she liked best about your work, which parts were difficult to understand, and ways in which your work could be improved. Reread your paper considering your critic's comments, and make the corrections you think are necessary.

PROOFREADING

Do a final proofreading of your paper double-checking your grammar, spelling, organization, and the clarity of your ideas.

LESSON TEN

Objectives
1. To complete the prereading and vocabulary work for chapters 21-24
2. To read chapters 21-24
3. To review the main ideas and events from chapters 21-24

Activities

Give students about fifteen minutes to preview the study questions and do the related vocabulary work for chapters 21-24. Have students read the chapters silently and answer the study questions. Then discuss the study questions for chapters 21-24.

LESSON ELEVEN

Objective

To discuss *Frankenstein* at the interpretive and critical levels

Activity 1

Choose the questions from the Extra Writing Assignments/Discussion Questions which seem most appropriate for your students. A class discussion of these questions is most effective is students have been given the opportunity to formulate answers to the questions prior to the discussion. To this end, you may either have all the students formulate answers to the questions, divide the class into groups and assign one or more questions to each group, or you could assign one question to each student in your class. The option you choose will make a difference in the amount of class time needed for this activity.

Activity 2

After students have had ample time to formulate answers to the questions, begin your class discussion of the questions and the ideas presented by the questions. Be sure students take notes during the discussion so they have information to study for the unit test.

EXTRA DISCUSSION QUESTIONS/WRITING ASSIGNMENTS - *Frankenstein*

Interpretive
1. From what point of view is this story told? How would the story change if told from only one character's point of view?

2. Discuss the creature's views on society, justice, and injustice.

3. Discuss the main themes in the novel.

4. What role does weather have in maintaining the mood in *Frankenstein*?

5. Why did Shelley include Dr. Darwin's name in the preface?

6. Discuss the type of families portrayed in the novel.

7. Discuss Victor Frankenstein's personality.

8. Discuss the creature's personality.

9. Discuss the use of emotions in the novel.

10. Discuss the symbolism behind Victor Frankenstein's crime against nature.

11. What role did Elizabeth play in the novel?

Critical
12. What reaction does the creature's appearance arouse in the reader?

13. Discuss the elements of the gothic novel in relation to *Frankenstein*.

14. Did Mary Shelley effectively use nature in her novel?

15. What is foreshadowing? Discuss the use of foreshadowing in the novel.

16. How does the author seem to feel about Victor? About the creature?

17. Explain the significance of the sub-title "The Modern Prometheus."

Frankenstein Extra Discussion Questions page 2

Personal Response
18. How did the epistolary style of the novel affect your understanding/enjoyment of it?

19. Do you think Mrs. Saville ever received the letters? Why or why not?

20. If you were Mary Shelley's editor, what changes would you suggest?

21. Would you recommend this book to a friend?

22. How did you feel about Victor Frankenstein as a person?

23. How did you feel about the creature?

24. In the Introduction, Mary Shelley said she wanted to "think of a story that would speak to the mysterious fears of our nature and waken thrilling horror." In your opinion, did she succeed? Why or why not?

25. Did you like the ending of the novel? Why or why not?

26. If you have a favorite horror story or movie, compare and contrast it with *Frankenstein*.

Quotations
1. "And now, once again, I bid my hideous progeny go forth and prosper. I have an affection for it, for it was the offspring of happy days, when death and grief were but words, which found no true echo in my heart."

2. "So strange an accident has happened to us, that I cannot forbear recording it, although it is very probable that you will see me before these papers can come into your possession."

3. "On perceiving me, the stranger addressed me in English, although with a foreign accent. "Before I come on board your vessel," said he, "will you have the kindness to inform me whither you are bound?"

4. "I have described myself as always having been imbued with a fervent longing to penetrate the secrets of nature."

5. "None but those who have experienced them can conceive of the enticements of science. In other studies you go as far as others have gone before you, and there is nothing more to know; but in a scientific pursuit there is continual food for discovery and wonder."

6. "Who shall conceive the horrors of my secret toil, as I dabbled among he unhallowed damps of the grave, or tortured the living animal to animate the lifeless clay?"

7. "I had desired it with an ardent fervor that far exceeded moderation; but now that I had finished, the beauty of the dream vanished, and breathless horror and disgust filled my heart."

8. "My dear Frankenstein, how glad I am to see you! How fortunate that you should be here at the very moment of my alighting!"

9. "Get well, and return to us. You will find a happy, cheerful home and friends who love you dearly."

10. "During the whole of this wretched mockery of justice I suffered living torture. It was to be decided, whether the course of my curiosity and lawless devices would cause the death of two of my fellow-beings: one a smiling babe, full of innocence and joy; the other far more dreadfully murdered, with every aggravation of infamy that could make the murder memorable in horror."

11. "But is it not a duty to the survivors, that we should refrain from augmenting their unhappiness by an appearance of immoderate grief? It is also a duty owed to yourself; for excessive sorrow prevents improvement or enjoyment, or event he discharge of daily usefulness, without which no man is fit for society."

12. "It is with considerable difficulty that I remember the original era of my being; all the events of that period appear confused and indistinct. A strange multiplicity of sensations seized me, and I saw, felt, heard, and smelt, at the same time."

13. "Accursed creator! Why did you form a monster so hideous that even you turned from me in disgust? God, in pit, made man beautiful and alluring, after his own image,; but my form is a filthy type of yours, more horrid even from the very resemblance. Satan had his companions, fellow-devils, to admire and encourage him; but I am solitary and abhorred."

14. "I was like a wild beast that had broken the toils; destroying the objects that obstructed me and ranging through the wood with a stag-like swiftness."

15. "I, too, can create desolation; my enemy is not invulnerable; this death will carry despair to him, and a thousand other miseries shall torment and destroy him."

16. "I am malicious because I am miserable. Am I not shunned and hated by all mankind?"

17. "I swear by the sun, and by the blue sky of Heaven, and by the fire of love that burns my heart, that if you grant my prayer, while they exist you shall never behold me again."

18. "I had rather be with you in your solitary rambles, than with these Scotch people whom I do not know; hasten the, my dear friend, to return, that I may again feel myself somewhat at home, which I cannot do in your absence."

19. "I confess to you, my friend, that I love you, and that in my airy dreams of futurity you have been my constant friend and companion."

20. ". . . and if I see but one smile on your lips when we meet, occasioned by this or any other exertion of mine, I shall need no other happiness."

21. "Oh! Peace, peace, my love," replied I; "this night, and all will be safe; but this night is dreadful, very dreadful."

22. "But such is not my destiny; I must pursue and destroy the being to whom I gave existence; then my lot on earth will be fulfilled, and I may die."

23. "During these last days I have been occupied in examining my past conduct; nor do I find it blamable."

24. "Wretch!" I said, "It is well that you come here to whine over the desolation that you have made. You throw a torch into a pile of buildings, and when they are consumed, you sit among the ruins, and lament the fall. Hypocritical fiend!"

25. "Blasted as thou were, my agony was still superior to thine, for the bitter sting of remorse will not cease to rankle in my wounds until death shall close them forever."

LESSON TWELVE

Objectives
    1. To introduce Writing Assignment 3
    2. To give students time to work on the writing assignment

Activity
    Distribute copies of Writing Assignment 3. Discuss the directions in detail and give students ample time to complete the assignment.

LESSON THIRTEEN

Objectives
    1. To give students the opportunity to do research for their Nonfiction Assignment
    2. To assist students in the proper use of the school library

Activity
    Take your class to the library for the entire class period. Tell them they can have the time to work on their Nonfiction Assignment. Students who have completed the assignment can use the time to read for pleasure. If your students need a review of where to find things in the library, take a few minutes to give them that review.

WRITING ASSIGNMENT #3 - *Frankenstein*

PROMPT

The creature told Victor Frankenstein that all he really wanted was friendship. He felt misunderstood by the humans he met because of his grotesque appearance. As much as we like to believe otherwise, appearance is often a deciding factor in developing friendships.

The creature has asked you to be his friend. Your assignment is to write a letter to the creature. Describe your idea of friendship. Include what you would be like as a friend and what you expect from a friend in return.

PREWRITING

The first thing you need to do is jot down ideas about what friendship means to you. What qualities do you have that make a good friend? What qualities are you looking for in a friend? What are the positive aspects of being and having a friend? What are the difficult parts?

Put down all your thoughts and then go back and sort through them. You may want to organize this section into two separate paragraphs–one on being a friend and one on what you want from a friend. Combine ideas that are similar.

DRAFTING

In your introductory paragraph, state your philosophy about friendship. Follow this with a paragraph about the kind of friend you are and one about what you are looking for in a friend. Your concluding paragraph should summarize the main points of your letter. You can also invite the creature to respond to you if he thinks the two of you could become friends.

PROMPT

When you finish the rough draft of your paper, ask a student who sits near you to read it. After reading your rough draft, he\she should tell you what he\she liked best about your work, which parts were difficult to understand, and ways in which your work could be improved. Reread your paper considering your critic's comments, and make the corrections you think are necessary.

PROOFREADING

Do a final proofreading of your paper double-checking your grammar, spelling, organization, and the clarity of your ideas.

LESSON FOURTEEN

<u>Objectives</u>

To review all of the vocabulary work done in this unit

<u>Activity</u>

Choose one (or more) of the vocabulary review activities listed below and spend your class period as directed in the activity. Some of the materials for these review activities are located in the Vocabulary Resources section in this unit.

VOCABULARY REVIEW ACTIVITIES

1. Divide your class into two teams and have an old-fashioned spelling or definition bee.

2. Give each of your students (or students in groups of two, three or four) a *Frankenstein* Vocabulary Word Search Puzzle. The person (group) to find all of the vocabulary words in the puzzle first wins.

3. Give students a *Frankenstein* Vocabulary Word Search Puzzle without the word list. The person or group to find the most vocabulary words in the puzzle wins.

4. Use a *Frankenstein* Vocabulary Crossword Puzzle. Put the puzzle onto a transparency on the overhead projector (so everyone can see it), and do the puzzle together as a class.

5. Give students a *Frankenstein* Vocabulary Matching Worksheet to do.

6. Divide your class into two teams. Use the *Frankenstein* vocabulary words with their letters jumbled as a word list. Student 1 from Team A faces off against Student 1 from Team B. You write the first jumbled word on the board. The first student (1A or 1B) to unscramble the word wins the chance for his/her team to score points. If 1A wins the jumble, go to student 2A and give him/her a definition. He/she must give you the correct spelling of the vocabulary word which fits that definition. If he/she does, Team A scores a point, and you give student 3A a definition for which you expect a correctly spelled matching vocabulary word. Continue giving Team A definitions until some team member makes an incorrect response. An incorrect response sends the game back to the jumbled -word face off, this time with students 2A and 2B. Instead of repeating giving definitions to the first few students of each team, continue with the student after the one who gave the last incorrect response on the team. For example, if Team B wins the jumbled-word face-off, and student 5B gave the last incorrect answer for Team B, you would start this round of definition questions with student 6B, and so on. The team with the most points wins!

LESSON FIFTEEN

Objective
   To study in more detail some of the main characters in *Frankenstein*

Activity 1
   Divide your class into groups, one for each of the following:
   1. Victor Frankenstein
   2. The creature
   3. Elizabeth Lavenza
   4. Alphonse Frankenstein
   5. Henry Clerval
   6. M. DeLacey
   7. Felix DeLacey
   8. Justine Moritz
   9. Robert Walton
   10. Caroline Beaufort Frankenstein

   Each group should write down the characteristics of the character they are assigned. Then they should confer and form opinions about that character's role in the novel.

Activity 2
   Have a spokesperson from each group report the group's findings. Encourage the rest of the class to ask questions. If they disagree with the opinions of the reporting group, they must present evidence from the book to support their argument(s).
   You may want to have a large piece of paper on the chalkboard or bulletin board. Put the name of each of the characters at the top of the chart. Have a writer from each group record the characteristics of the group's character. Students with artistic ability could draw their interpretations of what the characters look like.

LESSON SIXTEEN

Objective
   To compare and contrast a movie version of *Frankenstein* with the novel

Activity
   There are several movie versions of *Frankenstein* available. Choose one that is appropriate for your class. Show the movie. Afterwards, discuss ways in which the movie and the novel were similar and different. Discuss the reasons for the differences. You may want the students to write a short comparison/contrast paper after this discussion.

LESSON SEVENTEEN

Objectives
> 1. To widen the breadth of students' knowledge about the topics discussed or touched upon in *Frankenstein*
> 2. To check students' non-fiction assignments

Activity

Ask each student to give a brief oral report about the nonfiction work he/she read for the nonfiction assignment. Your criteria for evaluating this report will vary depending on the level of your students. You may wish for students to give a complete report without using notes of any kind, or you may want students to read directly from a written report, or you may want to do something in between those two extremes. Just make students aware of your criteria in ample time for them to prepare their reports.

Start with one student's report. After that, ask if anyone else in the class has read on a topic related to the first student's report. If no one has, choose another student at random. After each report, be sure to ask if anyone has a report related to the one just completed. That will help keep a continuity during the discussion of the reports.

LESSON EIGHTEEN

Objective
  To review the main ideas presented in *Frankenstein*

Activity #1
  Choose one of the review games/activities included in this unit and spend your class period as outlined there. Some materials for these activities are located in the Unit Resources section of this unit.

Activity #2
  Remind students that the Unit Test will be in the next class meeting. Stress the review of the Study Guides and their class notes as a last minute, brush-up review for the unit test.

REVIEW GAMES/ACTIVITIES - *Frankenstein*

1. Ask the class to make up a unit test for *Frankenstein*. The test should have 4 sections: matching, true/false, short answer, and essay. Students may use 1/2 period to make the test and then swap papers and use the other 1/2 class period to take a test a classmate has devised (open book). You may want to use the unit test included in this unit or take questions from the students' unit tests to formulate your own test.

2. Take 1/2 period for students to make up true and false questions (including the answers). Collect the papers and divide the class into two teams. Draw a big tic-tac-toe board on the chalk board. Make one team X and one team O. Ask questions to each side, giving each student one turn. If the question is answered correctly, that students' team's letter (X or O) is placed in the box. If the answer is incorrect, no mark is placed in the box. The object is to get three marks in a row like tic-tac-toe. You may want to keep track of the number of games won for each team.

3. Take 1/2 period for students to make up questions (true/false and short answer). Collect the questions. Divide the class into two teams. You'll alternate asking questions to individual members of teams A & B (like in a spelling bee). The question keeps going from A to B until it is correctly answered, then a new question is asked. A correct answer does not allow the team to get another question. Correct answers are +2 points; incorrect answers are -1 point.

4. Have students pair up and quiz each other from their study guides and class notes.

5. Give students a *Frankenstein* crossword puzzle to complete.

6. Divide your class into two teams. Use the *Frankenstein* crossword words with their letters jumbled as a word list. Student 1 from Team A faces off against Student 1 from Team B. You write the first jumbled word on the board. The first student (1A or 1B) to unscramble the word wins the chance for his/her team to score points. If 1A wins the jumble, go to student 2A and give him/her a clue. He/she must give you the correct word which matches that clue. If he/she does, Team A scores a point, and you give student 3A a clue for which you expect another correct response. Continue giving Team A clues until some team member makes an incorrect response. An incorrect response sends the game back to the jumbled-word face off, this time with students 2A and 2B. Instead of repeating giving clues to the first few students of each team, continue with the student after the one who gave the last incorrect response on the team. For example, if Team B wins the jumbled-word face-off, and student 5B gave the last incorrect answer for Team B, you would start this round of clue questions with student 6B, and so on.

UNIT TESTS

SHORT ANSWER UNIT TEST 1 *Frankenstein*

I. Matching/Identify

____ 1. Victor Frankenstein
____ 2. Henry Clerval
____ 3. Elizabeth Lavenza
____ 4. Robert Walton
____ 5. Margaret Saville
____ 6. Justine Moritz
____ 7. William Frankenstein
____ 8. Felix De Lacey
____ 9. Alphonse Frankenstein
____ 10. Caroline Beaufort

A. unknowingly taught the creature to speak and read
B. wrongly executed for murder
C. Frankenstein family matriarch
D. rescued Frankenstein from Arctic ice
E. died of grief in his son's arms
F. Frankenstein's best friend
G. creature's first victim
H. creator of the creature
I. recipient of a series of letters from her brother
J. lived with Frankenstein family, married Victor

II. Short Answer

1. What natural phenomena influenced Frankenstein?

2. What happened to Frankenstein at the end of the story?

3. What happened to the creature at the end of the story?

Short Answer Unit Test 1 *Frankenstein* page 2

4. How did Robert Walton meet Victor Frankenstein?

5. What was Frankenstein's reaction when Justine was accused of William's murder?

6. What did the creature ask Frankenstein to do, and why?

7. What does the creature learn to do while living in the lean-to, and how does he learn this?

Short Answer Unit Test 1 *Frankenstein* page 3

8. How did the creature feel after he killed William?

9. Who were the other two people who were killed by the creature?

10. How did Frankenstein feel when his experiment succeeded and the creature came to life?

Short Answer Unit Test 1 *Frankenstein* page 4

III. Essay

Describe the original personality of the creature, and the changes that occurred over the course of the novel.

Short Answer Unit Test 1 *Frankenstein* page 5

IV. Vocabulary

Listen to the vocabulary words and spell them. After you have spelled all the words, go back and write down the definitions.

ANSWER KEY SHORT ANSWER UNIT TEST 1 *Frankenstein*

I. Matching/Identification

H	1. Victor Frankenstein	A.	beat the creature with a stick
F	2. Henry Clerval	B.	wrongly executed for murder
J	3. Elizabeth Lavenza	C.	Frankenstein family matriarch
D	4. Robert Walton	D.	rescued Frankenstein from Arctic ice
I	5. Margaret Saville	E.	died of grief in his son's arms
B	6. Justine Moritz	F.	Frankenstein's best friend
G	7. William Frankenstein	G.	creature's first victim
A	8. Felix De Lacey	H.	creator of the creature
E	9. Alphonse Frankenstein	I.	recipient of a series of letters from her brother
C	10. Caroline Beaufort	J.	lived with Frankenstein family, married Victor

II. Short Answer

1. What natural phenomena influenced Frankenstein?

    He watched a tree being hit by lightning during a storm. He became interested in the theories of electricity and galvanism.

2. What happened to Frankenstein at the end of the story?

    He died of natural causes while in the cabin on the ship.

3. What happened to the creature at the end of the story?

    He came into the cabin and saw the dead Frankenstein. He told Walton that he was going to travel to the far north and kill himself. We last see the creature as he floats away into the darkness on an ice raft.

4. How did Robert Walton meet Victor Frankenstein?

    He and the crew found Frankenstein stuck on a large piece of ice. They rescued him and brought him aboard their vessel.

5. What was Frankenstein's reaction when Justine was accused of William's murder?

    He was sure the creature had committed the murder. He was torn between wanting to save Justine and not wanting to reveal his horrible secret to anyone. He considered himself the real murderer.

6. What did the creature ask Frankenstein to do, and why?

    He asked Frankenstein to create a female for him. He said that he was malicious because he was unhappy, and that if he were content he would not bother any more humans.

Answer Key Short Answer Unit Test 1 *Frankenstein*

7. What does the creature learn to do while living in the lean-to, and how does he learn this?
    He learns to speak, and then to read, by observing and listening to the cottagers. He found a portmanteau that had several books in it, and he read them. He then read the letters that were in the pocket of the coat he had taken from Victor Frankenstein.

8. How did the creature feel after he killed William?
    He was delighted that he was able to create despair for his creator.

9. Who were the other two people who were killed by the creature?
    Henry Clerval and Elizabeth Lavenza Frankenstein were the other victims.

10. How did Frankenstein feel when his experiment succeeded and the creature came to life?
    He was horrified and disgusted.

SHORT ANSWER UNIT TEST 2 *Frankenstein*

I. Matching/Identification

____ 1. Victor Frankenstein
____ 2. Henry Clerval
____ 3. Elizabeth Lavenza
____ 4. Robert Walton
____ 5. Margaret Saville
____ 6. Justine Moritz
____ 7. William Frankenstein
____ 8. Felix De Lacey
____ 9. Alphonse Frankenstein
____ 10. Caroline Beaufort

A. Frankenstein's best friend
B. creature's first victim
C. Frankenstein family matriarch
D. recipient of a series of letters from her brother
E. unknowingly taught creature to speak and read
F. wrongly executed for murder
G. rescued Frankenstein from Arctic ice
H. died of grief in his son's arms
I. lived with Frankenstein family, married Victor
J. creator of the creature

II. Short Answer

1. What discussions influenced the development of Mary Shelley's idea for a story?

2. What was one of the themes of the writers who influenced Victor?

Short Answer Unit Test 2 *Frankenstein* page 2

3. What happened to Frankenstein at the end of the story?

4. What was Frankenstein's reaction when Justine was accused of William's murder?

5. In general, what was the reaction of the people the creature encountered?

6. Who were the creature's victims, and why were they chosen?

Short Answer Unit Test 2 *Frankenstein* page 3

7. What does the creature learn to do while living in the lean-to, and how does he learn this?

8. What goal was Victor pursuing while at the university in Inglostadt?

9. How did Robert Walton meet Victor Frankenstein?

10. What happened to the creature at the end of the story?

Short Answer Unit Test 2 *Frankenstein* page 4

III. Essay

Discuss the creature's views on society, justice, and injustice. Include any changes that occurred in his views over the course of the novel, and the reasons for these changes.

Short Answer Unit Test 2 *Frankenstein* page 5

IV. Vocabulary

Listen to the vocabulary words and spell them. After you have spelled all the words, go back and write down the definitions.

ANSWER KEY SHORT ANSWER UNIT TEST 2 *Frankenstein*

Use this matching test key for Short Answer Unit Test 2 and the Advanced Short Answer Test.

I. Matching/Identification

J	1.	Victor Frankenstein	A.	Frankenstein's best friend
A	2.	Henry Clerval	B.	creature's first victim
I	3.	Elizabeth Lavenza	C.	Frankenstein family matriarch
G	4.	Robert Walton	D.	recipient of a series of letters from her brother
D	5.	Margaret Saville	E.	unknowingly taught creature to speak and read
F	6.	Justine Moritz	F.	wrongly executed for murder
B	7.	William Frankenstein	G.	rescued Frankenstein from Arctic ice
E	8.	Felix De Lacey	H.	died of grief in his son's arms
H	9.	Alphonse Frankenstein	I.	lived with Frankenstein family, married Victor
C	10.	Caroline Beaufort	J.	creator of the creature

II. Short Answer

1. What discussions influenced the development of Mary Shelley's idea for a story?
    She was listening to her husband, Shelley, and Lord Byron talk about the nature of life, and the possibility of creating a creature.

2. What was one of the themes of the writers who influenced Victor?
    The authors he read wrote about raising ghosts or devils. He tried to mimic them.

3. What happened to Frankenstein at the end of the story?
    He died of natural causes while in the cabin on the ship.

4. What was Frankenstein's reaction when Justine was accused of William's murder?
    He was sure the creature had committed the murder. He was torn between wanting to save Justine and not wanting to reveal his horrible secret to anyone. He considered himself the real murderer.

5. In general, what was the reaction of the people the creature encountered?
    They were frightened and horrified. They all either ran away or tried to injure him.

6. Who were the creature's victims, and why were they chosen?
    The first was William Frankenstein, Victor's youngest brother. The next was Henry Clerval, Frankenstein's best friend. The last was his bride, Elizabeth. They were all chosen to create despair in the life of Victor. Henry and Elizabeth were also killed in revenge because Frankenstein backed out on his promise to create a female for the creature.

7. What does the creature learn to do while living in the lean-to, and how does he learn this?
    He learns to speak, and then to read, by observing and listening to the cottagers. He found a portmanteau that had several books in it, and he read them. He then read the letters that were in the pocket of the coat he had taken from Victor Frankenstein.

8. What goal was Victor pursuing while at the university in Inglostadt?
    He wanted to try to renew life in a corpse, "to bestow animation upon lifeless matter."

9. How did Robert Walton meet Victor Frankenstein?
    He and the crew found Frankenstein stuck on a large piece of ice. They rescued him and brought him aboard their vessel.

10. What happened to the creature at the end of the story?
    He came into the cabin and saw the dead Frankenstein. He told Walton that he was going to travel to the far north and kill himself. We last see the creature as he floats away into the darkness on an ice raft.

ADVANCED SHORT ANSWER UNIT TEST *Frankenstein*

I. Matching/Identification

____ 1. Victor Frankenstein   A. Frankenstein's best friend
____ 2. Henry Clerval   B. creature's first victim
____ 3. Elizabeth Lavenza   C. Frankenstein family matriarch
____ 4. Robert Walton   D. recipient of a series of letters from her brother
____ 5. Margaret Saville   E. unknowingly taught creature to speak and read
____ 6. Justine Moritz   F. wrongly executed for murder
____ 7. William Frankenstein   G. rescued Frankenstein from Arctic ice
____ 8. Felix De Lacey   H. died of grief in his son's arms
____ 9. Alphonse Frankenstein   I. lived with Frankenstein family, married Victor
____ 10. Caroline Beaufort   J. creator of the creature

II. Short Answer

1. Discuss the role of nature in the novel.

2. Discuss Victor Frankenstein's personality.

Advanced Short Answer Unit Test *Frankenstein* page 2

3. Discuss each of the elements of the gothic novel and its relationship to *Frankenstein*.

4. Describe the original personality of the creature, and the changes that occurred over the course of the novel.

5. Describe and discuss the portrayal of families in *Frankenstein*.

Advanced Short Answer Unit Test *Frankenstein* page 3

III. Quotations
   Identify the speaker and discuss the significance of each of the following quotations.

1. "I have described myself as always having been imbued with a fervent longing to penetrate the secrets of nature."

2. "I had desired it with an ardour that far exceeded moderation; but now that I had finished, the beauty of the dream vanished, and breathless horror and disgust filled my heart."

3. "Accursed creator! Why did you form a monster so hideous that even you turned from me in disgust? God, in pit, made man beautiful and alluring, after his own image,; but my form is a filthy type of yours, more horrid even from the very resemblance. Satan had his companions, fellow-devils, to admire and encourage him; but I am solitary and abhorred."

Advanced Short Answer Test *Frankenstein* page 4

4. "I, too, can create desolation; my enemy is not invulnerable; this death will carry despair to him, and a thousand other miseries shall torment and destroy him."

5. "Wretch!" I said,"It is well that you come here to whine over the desolation that you have made. You throw a torch into a pile of buildings, and when they are consumed, you sit among the ruins, and lament the fall. Hypocritical fiend!"

Advanced Short Answer Test *Frankenstein* page 5

IV. Vocabulary

Listen to the vocabulary words and write them down. After you have written down all of the words, write a paragraph in which you use all the words. The paragraph must in some way relate to *Frankenstein*.

MULTIPLE CHOICE UNIT TEST 1 *Frankenstein*

I. Matching/Identification

____ 1. Victor Frankenstein   A. recipient of a series of letters from her brother
____ 2. Henry Clerval   B. creator of the creature
____ 3. Elizabeth Lavenza   C. Frankenstein family matriarch
____ 4. Robert Walton   D. creature's first victim
____ 5. Margaret Saville   E. lived with Frankenstein family, married Victor
____ 6. Justine Moritz   F. died of grief in his son's arms
____ 7. William Frankenstein   G. rescued Frankenstein from Arctic ice
____ 8. Felix De Lacey   H. unknowingly taught the creature to read and write
____ 9. Alphonse Frankenstein   I. Frankenstein's best friend
____ 10. Caroline Beaufort   J. wrongly executed for murder

II. Multiple Choice

1. True or False: Frankenstein was one of the sailors on Robert Walton's expedition.
    A. True
    B. False

2. What natural phenomena influenced Frankenstein?
    A. It was an avalanche.
    B. It was a waterfall.
    C. It was lightning.
    D. It was a tornado.

3. How did Frankenstein feel when his experiment succeeded, and the creature came to life?
    A. He was thrilled.
    B. He was horrified and disgusted.
    C. He was excited, but scared.
    D. He felt omnipotent.

4. True or False: Frankenstein was torn between wanting to save the accused and not wanting to reveal his horrible secret to anyone.
    A. True
    B. False

Multiple Choice Unit Test 1 *Frankenstein* page 2

5. How did the creature learn to speak and to read?
    A. He observed and listened to the De Laceys talking and reading.
    B. Frankenstein had programmed his brain to know how immediately.
    C. He sat outside the local school house and listened.
    D. A young child befriended him and taught him.

6. True or False: The creature was delighted that he was able to create despair for his creator.
    A. True
    B. False

7. True or False: The creature asked Frankenstein to teach him how to create another life.
    A. True
    B. False

8. True or False: The creature strangled Victor Frankenstein.
    A. True
    B. False

9. What happened to the creature at the end of the novel?
    A. He broke his neck as he tried to jump from the ship.
    B. He laughed and said he would continue to seek vengeance on humanity.
    C. He floated away into the darkness on an ice raft.
    D. Walton shot and killed him.

10. What happened on Frankenstein and Elizabeth's wedding night?
    A. The creature kidnapped Elizabeth.
    B. The creature attacked Victor, but Frankenstein managed to escape.
    C. The creature attacked both of them, but only killed Elizabeth.
    D. The creature broke into the room and killed Elizabeth.

Multiple Choice Unit Test 1 *Frankenstein* page 3

III. Quotations
Identify the speaker:

A. Victor Frankenstein	B. Robert Walton	C. The creature
D. Elizabeth	E. Alphonse Frankenstein	F. Henry Clerval

1. "So strange an accident has happened to us, that I cannot forbear recording it, although it is very probable that you will see me before these papers can come into your possession."

2. "Before I come on board your vessel, will you have the kindness to inform me whither you are bound?

3. "I have described myself as always having been imbued with a fervent longing to penetrate the secrets of nature."

4. "I had desired it with an ardent fervor that far exceeded moderation; but now that I had finished, the beauty of the dream vanished, and breathless horror and disgust filled my heart."

5. "Get well, and return to us. You will find a happy, cheerful home and friends who love you dearly."

6. "But is it not a duty to the survivors, that we should refrain from augmenting their unhappiness by an appearance of immoderate grief?"

7. "It is with considerable difficulty that I remember the original era of my being; all the events of that period appear confused and indistinct. A strange multiplicity of sensations seized me, and I saw, felt, heard, and smelt, at the same time."

8. "I swear by the sun, and by the blue sky of Heaven, and by the fire of love that burns my heart, that if you grant my prayer, while they exist you shall never behold me again."

9. "I had rather be with you in your solitary rambles, than with these Scotch people whom I do not know; hasten the, my dear friend, to return, that I may again feel myself somewhat at home, which I cannot do in your absence."

10. "I confess to you, my friend, that I love you, and that in my airy dreams of futurity you have been my constant friend and companion."

Multiple Choice Unit Test 1 *Frankenstein* page 4

IV. Vocabulary Matching

1. dilate
2. progeny
3. capacious
4. emaciated
5. penury
6. countenance
7. wantonly
8. obliterated
9. immutable
10. inexorable
11. debilitated
12. exhortations
13. abhorrent
14. sanguinary
15. indolence
16. sophisms
17. retrospect
18. satiated
19. conflagration
20. sustenance

A. face
B. weakened
C. believable but misleading arguments
D. means of nourishment
E. expand
F. a great fire
G. offspring, children
H. immorally, cruelly
I. urgings
J. looking back on the past
K. relentless, unyielding
L. fully satisfied
M. spacious, roomy
N. laziness
O. extreme poverty
P. bloody
Q. destroyed completely
R. thin and wasted
S. hateful, despicable
T. unchanging

MULTIPLE CHOICE UNIT TEST 2 *Frankenstein*

I. Matching/ Identification

____ 1. Victor Frankenstein   A. creator of the creature
____ 2. Henry Clerval   B. rescued Frankenstein from Arctic ice
____ 3. Elizabeth Lavenza   C. unknowingly taught the creature to read and write
____ 4. Robert Walton   D. recipient of a series of letters from her brother
____ 5. Margaret Saville   E. creature's first victim
____ 6. Justine Moritz   F. Frankenstein family matriarch
____ 7. William Frankenstein   G. Frankenstein's best friend
____ 8. Felix De Lacey   H. died of grief in his son's arms
____ 9. Alphonse Frankenstein   I. lived with Frankenstein family, married Victor
____ 10. Caroline Beaufort   J. wrongly executed for murder

II. Multiple Choice

1. True or False: The creature strangled Victor Frankenstein.
    A. True
    B. False

2. What threat did the creature make when Frankenstein backed out on their agreement?
    A. He said, "All of mankind is now cursed."
    B. He said, "I will pursue you to the ends of the earth and the end of your life."
    C. He said, "I will be with you on your wedding night."
    D. He said, "Alas, I am doomed to a wretched life on this earth!"

3. How did the creature learn to speak and to read?
    A. He observed and listened to the cottagers.
    B. Frankenstein had programmed his brain to know how immediately.
    C. He sat outside the local school house and listened.
    D. A young child befriended him and taught him.

4. What two major events happened to Frankenstein when he was seventeen?
    A. His youngest brother was born and he fell in love.
    B. He received his inheritance and traveled abroad.
    C. His mother died and he went to the university at Inglostadt to study.
    D. He got his first job and moved to his own apartment.

Multiple Choice Unit Test 2 *Frankenstein* page 2

5. True or False: At first, the creature felt confused because of all of the new sensations of life.
   A. True
   B. False

6. What happened to the creature at the end of the novel?
   A. He broke his neck as he tried to jump from the ship.
   B. He laughed and said he would continue to seek vengeance on humanity.
   C. He floated away into the darkness on an ice raft.
   D. Walton shot and killed him.

7. True or False: Frankenstein was torn between wanting to save the accused and not wanting to reveal his horrible secret to anyone.
   A. True
   B. False

8. True or False: The authors Frankenstein enjoyed talking about the life of the soul in heaven.
   A. True
   B. False

9. What discussions between Byron and Shelley influenced the development of Mary Shelley's idea for her novel?
   A. They were discussing Greek and Roman mythology.
   B. They were discussing the book of Genesis.
   C. They were discussing the nature of life.
   D. They were discussing the recent discovery of fossil remains of early humans.

10. True or False: Frankenstein wanted to try to create life in a test tube.
    A. True
    B. False

Multiple Choice Unit Test 2 *Frankenstein* page 3

III. Quotations
Identify the speaker

A. Victor Frankenstein   B. Robert Walton   C. The creature
D. Elizabeth   E. Alphonse Frankenstein   F. Henry Clerval

1. "I swear by the sun, and by the blue sky of Heaven, and by the fire of love that burns my heart, that if you grant my prayer, while they exist you shall never behold me again."

2. "Excessive sorrow prevents improvement or enjoyment, or even the discharge of daily usefulness, without such no man is fit for society."

3. "I was like a wild beast that had broken the toils; destroying the objects that obstructed me and ranging through the wood with a stag-like swiftness."

4. "Blasted as thou were, my agony was still superior to thine, for the bitter sting of remorse will not cease to rankle in my wounds until death shall close them forever."

5. "I am malicious because I am miserable. Am I not shunned and hated by all mankind?"

6. ". . . and if I see but one smile on your lips when we meet, occasioned by this or any other exertion of mine, I shall need no other happiness."

7. "Wretch!" I said,"It is well that you come here to whine over the desolation that you have made. You throw a torch into a pile of buildings, and when they are consumed, you sit among the ruins, and lament the fall. Hypocritical fiend!"

8. "I had desired it with an ardent fervor that far exceeded moderation; but now that I had finished, the beauty of the dream vanished, and breathless horror and disgust filled my heart."

9. "My dear Frankenstein, how glad I am to see you! How fortunate that you should be here at the very moment of my alighting!"

10. "None but those who have experienced them can conceive of the enticements of science. In other studies you go as far as others have gone before you, and there is nothing more to know; but in a scientific pursuit there is continual food for discovery and wonder."

Multiple Choice Unit Test 2 *Frankenstein* page 4

IV. Vocabulary Matching

1.	timorous	A.	destruction of life
2.	ignominious	B.	domineering
3.	vacillating	C.	steep
4.	physiognomy	D.	increased
5.	indefatigable	E.	passionate, enthusiastic
6.	cursory	F.	tireless
7.	paroxysm	G.	fluctuating, wavering
8.	ardent	H.	storminess
9.	posterity	I.	irritating
10.	detrimental	J.	harmful, damaging
11.	augmented	K.	hastily done
12.	benevolent	L.	disgraceful
13.	commiserate	M.	predict
14.	precipitous	N.	future generations
15.	expedient	O.	suitable, practical
16.	rankling	P.	spasm, convulsion
17.	imperious	Q.	feel or express sympathy for
18.	portend	R.	facial features with regard to revealing character
19.	inclemency	S.	generous
20.	carnage	T.	fearful

ANSWER SHEET Multiple Choice Unit Test *Frankenstein*

I. Matching

1. _____
2. _____
3. _____
4. _____
5. _____
6. _____
7. _____
8. _____
9. _____
10. _____

II. Multiple Choice

1. (A) (B) (C) (D)
2. (A) (B) (C) (D)
3. (A) (B) (C) (D)
4. (A) (B) (C) (D)
5. (A) (B) (C) (D)
6. (A) (B) (C) (D)
7. (A) (B) (C) (D)
8. (A) (B) (C) (D)
9. (A) (B) (C) (D)
10. (A) (B) (C) (D)

III. Quotations

1. _____
2. _____
3. _____
4. _____
5. _____
6. _____
7. _____
8. _____
9. _____
10. _____

IV. Vocabulary

1. _____
2. _____
3. _____
4. _____
5. _____
6. _____
7. _____
8. _____
9. _____
10. _____
11. _____
12. _____
13. _____
14. _____
15. _____
16. _____
17. _____
18. _____
19. _____
20. _____

ANSWER SHEET KEY Multiple Choice Unit Test 1 *Frankenstein*

I. Matching

1. __B__
2. __I__
3. __E__
4. __G__
5. __A__
6. __J__
7. __D__
8. __H__
9. __F__
10. __C__

II. Multiple Choice

1. (A)(   )(C)(D)
2. (A)(B)(   )(D)
3. (A)(   )(C)(D)
4. (   )(B)(C)(D)
5. (   )(B)(C)(D)
6. (   )(B)(C)(D)
7. (A)(   )(C)(D)
8. (A)(   )(C)(D)
9. (A)(B)(   )(D)
10. (A)(B)(C)(   )

III. Quotations

1. __B__
2. __A__
3. __A__
4. __A__
5. __D__
6. __E__
7. __C__
8. __C__
9. __F__
10. __D__

IV. Vocabulary

1. __E__
2. __G__
3. __M__
4. __R__
5. __O__
6. __A__
7. __H__
8. __Q__
9. __T__
10. __K__
11. __B__
12. __I__
13. __S__
14. __P__
15. __N__
16. __C__
17. __J__
18. __L__
19. __F__
20. __D__

ANSWER SHEET KEY Multiple Choice Unit Test 2 *Frankenstein*

I. Matching

1. __A__
2. __G__
3. __I__
4. __B__
5. __D__
6. __J__
7. __E__
8. __C__
9. __H__
10. __F__

II. Multiple Choice

1. (A)(   )(C)(D)
2. (A)(B)(   )(D)
3. (   )(B)(C)(D)
4. (A)(B)(   )(D)
5. (   )(B)(C)(D)
6. (A)(B)(   )(D)
7. (   )(B)(C)(D)
8. (A)(   )(C)(D)
9. (A)(B)(   )(D)
10. (A)(   )(C)(D)

III. Quotations

1. __C__
2. __E__
3. __C__
4. __C__
5. __C__
6. __D__
7. __B__
8. __C__
9. __F__
10. __D__

IV. Vocabulary

1. __T__
2. __L__
3. __G__
4. __R__
5. __F__
6. __K__
7. __P__
8. __E__
9. __N__
10. __J__
11. __D__
12. __S__
13. __Q__
14. __C__
15. __O__
16. __I__
17. __B__
18. __M__
19. __H__
20. __K__

UNIT RESOURCE MATERIALS

BULLETIN BOARD IDEAS - *Frankenstein*

1. Save one corner of the board for the best of students' *Frankenstein* writing assignments.

2. Draw one of the word search puzzles onto the bulletin board. (Be sure to enlarge it.) Write the key words to one side. Invite students to take their pens or markers and find the words before and/or after class (or perhaps this could be an activity for students who finish their work early).

3. Have students illustrate characters in the book and include information gained from the novel describing them.

4. Invite students to help make an interactive bulletin board quiz. Give each student a half-sheet of paper folded in half so that it can open. On the outside flap, have each student write a description of one of the characters in the text. On the inside, students will write the name of that character. Staple or tack the papers to the bulletin board so that students can lift the flaps to see the answers.

5. Collect pictures of the cities mentioned in the book and make a display.

6. Make a display of pictures of book jackets and artwork from the various editions of *Frankenstein* You may want to include pictures from the many movies about *Frankenstein.*

7. Make a display of travel posters of Switzerland, Germany, Russia, and the Arctic.

8. Display articles about Mary Shelley and critiques of her work.

9. Have students design postcards depicting settings of the book.

10. Display a large map of Europe and have students mark the route that Victor Frankenstein took while pursuing the creature to the Arctic.

EXTRA ACTIVITIES - *Frankenstein*

One of the difficulties in teaching a novel is that all students don't read at the same speed. One student who likes to read may take the book home and finish it in a day or two. Sometimes a few students finish the in-class assignments early. The problem, then, is finding suitable extra activities for students.

One thing you can do is to keep a little library in the classroom. For this unit on *Frankenstein*, you might check out from the school library other books by Mary Shelley. There are also many other Gothic novels that students would enjoy reading. Several journals have critiques of Mary Shelley's works. Some students may enjoy reading these and responding either in writing or in discussion groups.

This novel is available on audio tape in both abridged and non-abridged versions. Your students who have reading difficulties or speak English as a second language may benefit from listening to all or part of the book on tape.

Mary Shelley led a quite interesting, if rather unusual life. Your students may enjoy reading a biography of her and of her husband, Percy Shelley. Some critics think that the events in *Frankenstein* strongly parallel the events in Mary Shelley's own life. Your more able students may want to read her biography and compare the events in her life with those in the novel.

Other things you may keep on hand are puzzles. We have made some relating directly to *Frankenstein* for you. Feel free to duplicate them for your students.

Some students may like to draw. You might devise a contest or allow some extra-credit grade for students who draw characters or scenes from *Frankenstein*. Note, too, that if the students do not want to keep their drawings you may pick up some extra bulletin board materials this way. If you have a contest and you supply the prize or, you could possibly make the drawing itself a non-refundable entry fee.

The pages which follow contain games, puzzles and worksheets. The keys, when appropriate, immediately follow the puzzle or worksheet. There are two main groups of activities: one group for the unit; that is, generally relating to the *Frankenstein* text, and another group of activities related strictly to the *Frankenstein* vocabulary.

Directions for the games, puzzles and worksheets are self-explanatory. The object here is to provide you with extra materials you may use in any way you choose.

MORE ACTIVITIES - *Frankenstein*

1. Pick a chapter or scene with a great deal of dialogue and have the students act it out on a stage. (Perhaps you could assign various scenes to different groups of students so more than one scene could be acted and more students could participate.)

2. Have students design a book cover (front and back and inside flaps) for *Frankenstein*.

3. Have students design a bulletin board (ready to put up; not just sketched) for *Frankenstein*.

4. Invite a story teller to tell one or more stories related to *Frankenstein* in class.

5. Help students design and produce a talk show. Choose one of the story incidents as the topic. The host will interview the various characters. (Students should make up the questions they want the host to ask the character(s).)

6. Have students work in pairs to create an interview with one of the characters. One student should be the interviewer and the other should be the interviewee. Students can work together to compose questions for the interviewer to ask. Each pair of students could present their interview to the class.

7. Invite students who have read other books by Mary Shelley or other Gothic novels to make presentations about their reading to the class.

8. Mary Shelley's parents and husband were all writers. her mother, Mary Wollenstonecraft Godwin, wrote a famous work for the early feminist cause titled *A Vindication of the Rights of Women* (1792). Her father, William Godwin, wrote *Political Justice* (1793) and *Caleb Williams* (1794). Her husband, Percy Shelley, was a noted poet. His most famous work was *Prometheus Unbound*. Invite students who have read works by any of these writers to present bookmarks to the class.

9. Have a contest to name the creature.

10. It is not clear what happened to the creature after he rowed away from Walton's ship. Have students work in small groups to write a sequel telling what happened to the creature.

WORD SEARCH - Frankenstein

Words are placed backwards, forward, diagonally, up and down. Words listed below are included in the maze. Circle the hidden vocabulary words in the maze.

```
F D V N S P S C P K C M L V H Q L R B K
E R U T A E R C I N G O L S T A D T K R
K T A N S Y T Z A C V L R T A Z Q D R H
G V D N N R P N G R E A Z N V Y P T E Z
G H V P K N F E S E L C R Q E D X H M L
R U L I F E E S R O M E R K N L R B P J
E C I G C H N H E C G Y T A E H I I E T
A A W L F T T S T I Y X L J G Q H U N V
D R E A T A O Y T D N T S U G S I D S Q
E O N R L Y L R E E O N Y G D K A Z D H
L L G C B D X P L C I R O N S H C F L B
I I L T W Y M E S F A N E C U H G O I D
Z N A I I A R A R M E I R K E F P B G E
A E N C L D L O N N R L J M H N J S H S
B L D T L Z Z T N F E E I R T T T E T M
E K V N I D H O O V S S Q X E T F R H F
T I X Z A Y I Q W N T C T K M M O V C Q
H R F G M S Y R O R Z G C B O C O A C F
P W J J U N F H Y T M O T N R H D T D C
H I C F H M P F I S L D L Y P N E I H Y
P N N V J L Z R L G Z S D T W L Z O C D
V O T F A M O R Q M N G T T A Q X N R L
C R D W V M T N D X R Y R M T B N G C V
D T D X H M K Z Q C D P E M N X S J L L
D P T F X P C V W B Y F C Y Y D B X X F
```

ALPHONSE	DISGUST	GENEVA	LIFE	REMORSE
ALPS	ELIZABETH	GUILTY	LIGHT	SAFIE
ARCTIC	ENGLAND	HENRY	LOCKET	SCARLET
BYRON	ERNEST	INGOLSTADT	MARY	SCOTLAND
CAROLINE	FELIX	INNOCENT	MORITZ	THREE
CHEMISTRY	FEMALE	KIRWIN	OBSERVATION	VICTOR
CONFUSION	FOOD	KREMPE	PERCY	WALDMAN
CORNELIUS	FRANKENSTEIN	LACEY	PROMETHEUS	WALTON
CREATURE	FRIENDSHIP	LETTERS	READ	WILLIAM

WORD SEARCH - Frankenstein

Words are placed backwards, forward, diagonally, up and down. Words listed below are included in the maze. Circle the hidden vocabulary words in the maze.

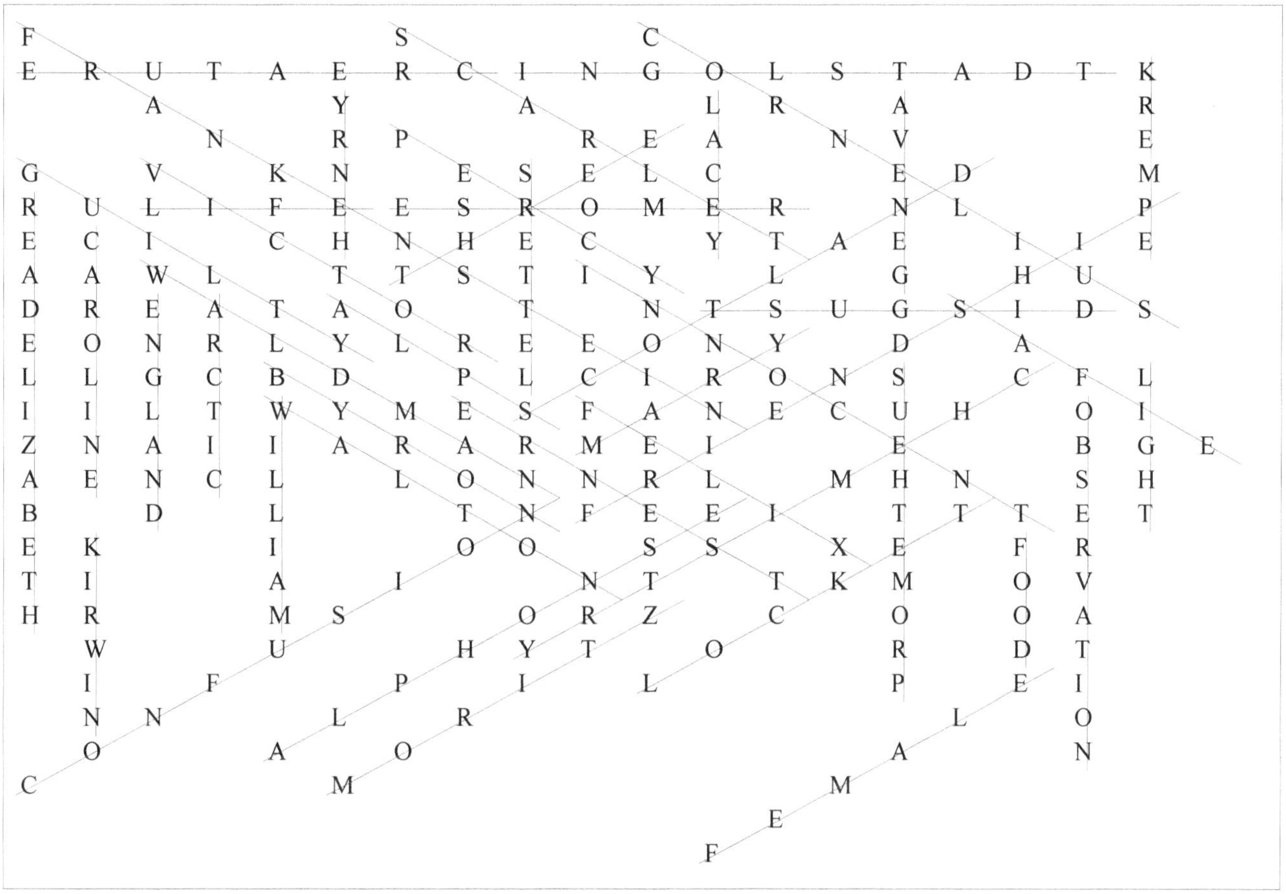

ALPHONSE	DISGUST	GENEVA	LIFE	REMORSE
ALPS	ELIZABETH	GUILTY	LIGHT	SAFIE
ARCTIC	ENGLAND	HENRY	LOCKET	SCARLET
BYRON	ERNEST	INGOLSTADT	MARY	SCOTLAND
CAROLINE	FELIX	INNOCENT	MORITZ	THREE
CHEMISTRY	FEMALE	KIRWIN	OBSERVATION	VICTOR
CONFUSION	FOOD	KREMPE	PERCY	WALDMAN
CORNELIUS	FRANKENSTEIN	LACEY	PROMETHEUS	WALTON
CREATURE	FRIENDSHIP	LETTERS	READ	WILLIAM

CROSSWORD - *Frankenstein*

CROSSWORD CLUES - *Frankenstein*

ACROSS

1 Verdict at Victor's trial
4 Creature's first feeling
6 Home of Frankenstein family
7 Left father to marry Felix
9 Incrimination evidence
12 Frankenstein's best friend; ___ Clerval
13 Frankenstein's feeling after creation
14 What Frankenstein wanted to create
16 Meeting site for creature and creator
17 What Felix taught creature to do
20 Miserable wretch
22 Number of creature's victims
26 The creator
27 Creature's request of Frankenstein
28 Author of Frankenstein; ___ Shelley
29 Wrongly executed; Justine ___
30 Creature asked for his friendship: M. De ___
31 Intended for Margaret Saville
32 Creature wanted this from humans
33 Frankenstein abandoned creation plans here

DOWN

2 Subject studied by Victor
3 Site of original creation
4 Frankenstein matriarch; ___ Beaufort
5 Taught Safie and the creature; ___ de Lacey
6 Verdict at Justine's trial
7 Killed Victor's mother; ___ fever
8 Hard for creature to find
10 Unfriendly professor
11 Proposed writing ghost stories; Lord ___
15 Married Victor; ___ Lavenza
16 Creature last seen here
18 Frankenstein compared to him
19 His discussions influenced his wife
20 Influential author; ___ Agrippa
21 Wanted military career; ___ Frankenstein
23 Frankenstein's feeling about Justine
24 Introduced Victor to natural philosophy
25 Friendly Irish magistrate

CROSSWORD ANSWER KEY - *Frankenstein*

MATCHING QUIZ/WORKSHEET 1 - *Frankenstein*

_____	1. Victor Frankenstein	A. Frankenstein's favorite professor
_____	2. Henry Clerval	B. Youngest member of Frankenstein family
_____	3. Elizabeth Lavenza	C. Site of creature's creation
_____	4. Robert Walton	D. Arctic explorer who rescued Frankenstein
_____	5. Margaret Saville	E. Frankenstein family home
_____	6. Justine Moritz	F. Site of first meeting between creature and creator
_____	7. William Frankenstein	G. Was killed on her wedding night
_____	8. Felix De Lacey	H. Wrongly executed for murder
_____	9. Alphonse Frankenstein	I. Recipient of letters from her brother
_____	10. Caroline Beaufort	J. Frankenstein went there to create female creature
_____	11. Ingolstadt	K. Creator of the creature
_____	12. Krempe	L. Victor's father
_____	13. Kirwin	M. Arabian wife of Felix
_____	14. Waldman	N. The novel begins and ends here
_____	15. Arctic	O. Victor Frankenstein's best friend
_____	16. Safie	P. Unpleasant professor
_____	17. Alps	Q. Died of scarlet fever
_____	18. Geneva	R. Was double-crossed by the Turk
_____	19. Scotland	S. Irish magistrate who aided Frankenstein
_____	20. England	T. Frankenstein went here to meet philosopher

MATCHING QUIZ/WORKSHEET 2 - *Frankenstein*

_____	1. Henry Clerval	A. Creature asked him for friendship
_____	2. Robert Walton	B. Loving mother of Frankenstein children
_____	3. Victor Frankenstein	C. Related story to his sister in letters
_____	4. Justine Moritz	D. Wanted a military career
_____	5. Caroline Beaufort	E. Innocent but pleaded guilty
_____	6. William Frankenstein	F. Full of disgust and horror for his work
_____	7. M. De Lacey	G. Frankenstein stopped second creation here
_____	8. Creature	H. Studied by Frankenstein
_____	9. Ingolstadt	I. Creature's dwelling
_____	10. Arctic	J. Introduced Frankenstein to natural philosophy
_____	11. Elizabeth Lavenza	K. Unknowingly taught creature to speak and read
_____	12. Ernest Frankenstein	L. His writings influenced Victor
_____	13. Cornelius Agrippa	M. Creature's first victim
_____	14. Felix De Lacey	N. Site of Victor's original creation
_____	15. Waldman	O. Misunderstood by humanity
_____	16. Chemistry	P. Left her father to marry Felix
_____	17. Hovel	Q. Nursed Victor through months of fever
_____	18. Safie	R. Site of first meeting of creator and creature
_____	19. Alps	S. Adopted and raised by Frankenstein family
_____	20. Scotland	T. Victor pursued the creature here

ANSWER KEYS: MATCHING WORKSHEETS - *Frankenstein*

	<u>1</u>	<u>2</u>
1.	K	Q
2.	O	C
3.	G	F
4.	D	E
5.	I	B
6.	H	M
7.	B	A
8.	R	O
9.	L	N
10.	Q	T
11.	C	S
12.	P	D
13.	S	L
14.	A	K
15.	N	J
16.	M	H
17.	F	I
18.	E	P
19.	J	R
20.	T	G

JUGGLE LETTER REVIEW GAME - *Frankenstein*

SCRAMBLED	WORD	CLUE
PLAS	ALPS	meeting site
ICTCRA	ARCTIC	creature last seen here
UIOCTEROANRFALEB	CAROLINE BEAUFORT	Frankenstein matriarch
SERHYMCIT	CHEMISTRY	studied by Victor
INSNOFCUO	CONFUSION	creature's first feeling
RSAELUPAPGIONCRI	CORNELIUS AGRIPPA	influential author
ETRRUAEC	CREATURE	miserable wretch
TSSDIUG	DISGUST	post-creation feeling
AEVLTHLABZEZNAEI	ELIZABETH LAVENZA	married Victor
NERSTE	ERNEST	wanted military career
IKNEAFTNRNES	FRANKENSTEIN	unfortunate Genevese family
XIFECEALLYED	FELIX DE LACEY	taught Safie and the creature
ODFO	FOOD	hard for creature to find
LYGTIU	GUILTY	verdict at Justine's trial
EHRCLVALEYNR	HENRY CLERVAL	nursed Victor through fever
DONLAISTTG	INGOLSTADT	site of original creation
CNTINNEO	INNOCENT	verdict at Victor's trial
IROMETSZUJNTI	JUSTINE MORITZ	wrongly executed
IINKWR	KIRWIN	friendly Irish magistrate
EEMRKP	KREMPE	unfriendly professor
HLTIG	LIGHT	initially irritating to the creature
ETOLKC	LOCKET	incrimination evidence
NOLYDORBR	LORD BYRON	proposed writing ghost stories
HLLRMAYEYSE	MARY SHELLEY	author of *Frankenstein*
YLLERHEPSYEC	PERCY SHELLEY	influential husband of author
YEMCELAD	M DE LACEY	creature wanted his friendship
STEOMEURPH	PROMETHEUS	Frankenstein compared to him
WAROONBRETLT	ROBERT WALTON	rescued Frankenstein
AEISF	SAFIE	left father to marry Felix
AETVFSRCRLEE	SCARLET FEVER	killed Victor's mother
LANDCTSO	SCOTLAND	second creation work here
TOIRCV	VICTOR	the creator
MLAANDW	WALDMAN	friendly professor
MILLIWA	WILLIAM	first victim

VOCABULARY RESOURCE MATERIALS

WORD SEARCH - Frankenstein Vocabulary

Words are placed backwards, forward, diagonally, up and down. Words listed below are included in the maze. Circle the hidden vocabulary words in the maze.

```
P A P P A L L I N G Y S A T I A T E D N
R L Z J P A G N M G L T H D F S X P I Q
E Z V R O T X D K M T E D J C U R P A D
C V D Z S N F V Q W U H K Z Z O H W B X
I S U S T E N A N C E T O B L I V I O N
P W Q S E M H Q P G G I A H X D C S L H
I R J H R I Z A P E M P K B S O A L I K
T E S P I R S M R P R E Y E L K R I C B
O T Y A T T N Q E R J D I M W E N N A J
U C N R Y E J R W B O R I F W D A T L R
S H E O L D I C F V E W Z T E J G E K J
P E G X J O B A F V R S I K I T E R P D
S D O Y U Y B P E M L A A N C O T M N Y
C U R S O R Y R A N K L I N G G N E L V
P M P M O J P I D D S U G Y G C T N R I
E R E P S P G C V E G B R Z Z R O T G V
N M T B W Y H E S T B R L T O T T N P H
U G A N Q T N I F N R I C P N N O E U V
R P L C V I G R S E D O L A E M P D R X
Y D I Y I M N X V M H U W I I D I R L T
O B D U R A T E V G S S D N T U D A O R
T W M B S L T N Y U H E I X G A T X I W
H R C B F A B E T A P O N N N L T F N L
W Q B K P C N C D X U G A T L B D E E C
I N D O L E N C E S P L M Z M G L X D X
```

APPALLING	DIABOLICAL	IMPERIOUS	PERDITION	SATIATED
ARDENT	DILATE	INDOLENCE	PORTEND	SLAKED
AUGMENTED	EMACIATED	INTERMENT	POSTERITY	SOPHISMS
CALAMITY	EPITHETS	LANGUID	PRECIPITOUS	SUSTENANCE
CAPRICE	EXPEDIENT	OBDURATE	PROGENY	WANTONLY
CARNAGE	FETTER	OBLIVION	PURLOINED	WRETCHED
CURSORY	HARROWING	ODIOUS	RANKLING	
DEBILITATED	IGNOMINIOUS	PAROXYSM	REVERIES	
DETRIMENTAL	IMMUTABLE	PENURY	SALUBRIOUS	

WORD SEARCH - Frankenstein Vocabulary

Words are placed backwards, forward, diagonally, up and down. Words listed below are included in the maze. Circle the hidden vocabulary words in the maze.

APPALLING	DIABOLICAL	IMPERIOUS	PERDITION	SATIATED
ARDENT	DILATE	INDOLENCE	PORTEND	SLAKED
AUGMENTED	EMACIATED	INTERMENT	POSTERITY	SOPHISMS
CALAMITY	EPITHETS	LANGUID	PRECIPITOUS	SUSTENANCE
CAPRICE	EXPEDIENT	OBDURATE	PROGENY	WANTONLY
CARNAGE	FETTER	OBLIVION	PURLOINED	WRETCHED
CURSORY	HARROWING	ODIOUS	RANKLING	
DEBILITATED	IGNOMINIOUS	PAROXYSM	REVERIES	
DETRIMENTAL	IMMUTABLE	PENURY	SALUBRIOUS	

VOCABULARY CROSSWORD - *Frankenstein*

VOCABULARY CROSSWORD CLUES - *Frankenstein*

ACROSS
1 Thin and wasted
3 Shocking
7 Distressing; agonizing
10 Extreme poverty
11 Hateful; detestable
13 Expand
16 Stubborn
17 Domineering
19 Healthful
25 Destroyed completely
26 Children; offspring
27 Abusive words

DOWN
1 Urges
2 Destruction or wreckage of life
3 Passionate; enthusiastic
4 Lacking energy
5 Unchanging
6 Misleading arguments
8 Laziness
9 Relentless; unyielding
12 Hateful
14 Whim
15 Means of nourishment
18 Shackle
20 Increased; added to
21 Forgotten
22 Fully satisfied
23 Spasm; convulsion
24 Quenched

VOCABULARY CROSSWORD ANSWER KEY - *Frankenstein*

VOCABULARY WORKSHEET 1 *Frankenstein*

Directions: Place the letter of the matching definition on the blank line.

_____ 1.	portend	A.	urgings
_____ 2.	wantonly	B.	facial features with regard to revealing character
_____ 3.	immutable	C.	a great fire
_____ 4.	harrowing	D.	extreme poverty
_____ 5.	expedient	E.	unchanging
_____ 6.	reveries	F.	thin and wasted
_____ 7.	dilate	G.	quenched
_____ 8.	carnage	H.	predicted
_____ 9.	repugnance	I.	laziness
_____ 10.	prognosticated	J.	complete ruin
_____ 11.	indolence	K.	means of nourishment
_____ 12.	perdition	L.	abusive words or phrases
_____ 13.	penury	M.	suitable, practical
_____ 14.	physiognomy	N.	loathing
_____ 15.	exhortations	O.	expand
_____ 16.	conflagration	P.	destruction of life
_____ 17.	epithets	Q.	predict
_____ 18.	sustenance	R.	daydreams
_____ 19.	slaked	S.	immorally, cruelly
_____ 20.	emaciated	T.	distressing

ANSWER KEY VOCABULARY WORKSHEET 1 Frankenstein

Directions: Place the letter of the matching definition on the blank line.

Q	1.	portend	A.	urgings
S	2.	wantonly	B.	facial features with regard to revealing character
E	3.	immutable	C.	a great fire
T	4.	harrowing	D.	extreme poverty
M	5.	expedient	E.	unchanging
R	6.	reveries	F.	thin and wasted
O	7.	dilate	G.	quenched
P	8.	carnage	H.	predicted
N	9.	repugnance	I.	laziness
H	10.	prognosticated	J.	complete ruin
I	11.	indolence	K.	means of nourishment
J	12.	perdition	L.	abusive words or phrases
D	13.	penury	M.	suitable, practical
B	14.	physiognomy	N.	loathing
A	15.	exhortations	O.	expand
C	16.	conflagration	P.	destruction of life
L	17.	epithets	Q.	predict
K	18.	sustenance	R.	daydreams
G	19.	slaked	S.	immorally, cruelly
F	20.	emaciated	T.	distressing

VOCABULARY WORKSHEET 2 Frankenstein

_____ 1. hateful
    A. benevolent   B. harrowing   C. odious   D. ignominious

_____ 2. spacious, roomy
    A. ardent   B. cursory   C. precipitous   D. capacious

_____ 3. miserable
    A. rankling   B. wretched   C. satiated   D. timorous

_____ 4. forgotten
    A. repugnance   B. penury   C. oblivion   D. capacious

_____ 5. whim
    A. caprice   B. calamity   C. conflagration   D. physiognomy

_____ 6. predicted
    A. augmented   B. prognosticated   C. obliterated   D. slaked

_____ 7. shackle
    A. progeny   B. commiserate   C. portend   D. fetter

_____ 8. healthful
    A. salubrious   B. ardent   C. emaciated   D. languid

_____ 9. complete ruin
    A. carnage   B. oblivion   C. perdition   D. penury

_____ 10. steep
    A. precipitous   B. diabolical   C. appalling   D. inexorable

_____ 11. weakened
    A. augmented   B. obliterated   C. satiated   D. debilitated

_____ 12. hateful, detestable
    A. purloined   B. abhorrent   C. indefatigable   D. indolence

_____ 13. immorally, cruelly
    A. vacillating   B. rankling   C. wantonly   D. detrimental

_____ 14. bloody
    A. sanguinary   B. conflagration   C. obdurate   D. odious

_____ 15. weary, listless
    A. capacious   B. expedient   C. retrospect   D. languid

_____ 16. disaster
    A. inclemency   B. calamity   C. paroxysm   D. epithets

_____ 17. burial
    A. countenance   B. caprice   C. perdition   D. interment

_____ 18. domineering
    A. debilitated   B. imperious   C. rankling   D. languid

_____ 19. devilish
    A. diabolical   B. inexorable   C. odious   D. detrimental

_____ 20. shocking
    A. emaciated   B. vacillating   C. appalling   D. wantonly

Answer Key Vocabulary Worksheet 2 *Frankenstein*

C	1.	hateful			
		A. benevolent	B. harrowing	C. **odious**	D. ignominious
D	2.	spacious, roomy			
		A. ardent	B. cursory	C. precipitous	D. **capacious**
B	3.	miserable			
		A. rankling	B. **wretched**	C. satiated	D. timorous
C	4.	forgotten			
		A. repugnance	B. penury	C. **oblivion**	D. capacious
A	5.	whim			
		A. **caprice**	B. calamity	C. conflagration	D. physiognomy
B	6.	predicted			
		A. augmented	B. **prognosticated**	C. obliterated	D. slaked
D	7.	shackle			
		A. progeny	B. commiserate	C. portend	D. **fetter**
A	8.	healthful			
		A. **salubrious**	B. ardent	C. emaciated	D. languid
C	9.	complete ruin			
		A. carnage	B. oblivion	C. **perdition**	D. penury
A	10.	steep			
		A. **precipitous**	B. diabolical	C. appalling	D. inexorable
D	11.	weakened			
		A. augmented	B. obliterated	C. satiated	D. **debilitated**
B	12.	hateful, detestable			
		A. purloined	B. **abhorrent**	C. indefatigable	D. indolence
C	13.	immorally, cruelly			
		A. vacillating	B. rankling	C. **wantonly**	D. detrimental
A	14.	bloody			
		A. **sanguinary**	B. conflagration	C. obdurate	D. odious
D	15.	weary, listless			
		A. capacious	B. expedient	C. retrospect	D. **languid**
B	16.	disaster			
		A. inclemency	B. **calamity**	C. paroxysm	D. epithets
D	17.	burial			
		A. countenance	B. caprice	C. perdition	D. **interment**
B	18.	domineering			
		A. debilitated	B. **imperious**	C. rankling	D. languid
A	19.	devilish			
		A. **diabolical**	B. inexorable	C. odious	D. detrimental
C	20.	shocking			
		A. emaciated	B. vacillating	C. **appalling**	D. wantonly

VOCABULARY JUGGLE LETTER REVIEW GAME *Frankenstein*

SCRAMBLED	WORD	CLUE
BNORTARHE	ABHORRENT	hateful, detestable
ANPLAILGP	APPALLING	shocking
DREATN	ARDENT	passionate, enthusiastic
EDNEAGMUT	AUGMENTED	increased
TNEVLNEOEB	BENEVOLENT	generous
TMYCALIA	CALAMITY	disaster
SPOIAUCAC	CAPACIOUS	spacious, roomy
PECCAIR	CAPRICE	whim
AEACGNR	CARNAGE	destruction of life
IACMSEOETMR	COMMISERATE	feel sympathy for
ANFORCNGOLAIT	CONFLAGRATION	a great fire
EUATOENNCNC	COUNTENANCE	face
ROSUYRC	CURSORY	hastily done
DTLBEIETIDA	DEBILITATED	weakened
ERNITADELMT	DETRIMENTAL	harmful, damaging
CAADIBOLLI	DIABOLICAL	devilish
TDELAI	DILATE	expand
DAIMEEATC	EMACIATED	thin and wasted
TIPHETES	EPITHETS	abusive words
TTINOARSOHXE	EXHORTATIONS	urgings
NEDTPEXIE	EXPEDIENT	suitable, practical
TTFREE	FETTER	shackle
IRGHNROAW	HARROWING	distressing, agonizing
RWIAHNGRO	IGNOMINIOUS	disgraceful
TUBMALEMI	IMMUTABLE	unchanging
SERIUOIPM	IMPERIOUS	domineering
EMYCEILCNN	INCLEMENCY	storminess
AGBIIDLEENFAT	INDEFATIGABLE	tireless
IOCLNEDNE	INDOLENCE	laziness
XEBLNEORIA	INEXORABLE	relentless, unyielding
REITTNEMN	INTERMENT	burial
NDGAIUL	LANGUID	languid
BUEDATOR	OBDURATE	stubborn
TLIETDORBAE	OBLITERATED	destroyed completely
VNBIOOLI	OBLIVION	forgetfulness
DIOUSO	ODIOUS	hateful
XRPMASOY	PAROXYSM	spasm, convulsion
RYPENU	PENURY	extreme poverty
NOITIDREP	PERDITION	complete ruin

OYHYNOIMGPS	PHYSIOGNOMY	facial features with regard to revealing character
RNEPDTO	PORTEND	predict
TPIOSYTER	POSTERITY	future generations
ICUISOTPREP	PRECIPITOUS	steep
EYPORGN	PROGENY	children, offspring
RGOTCTDPONSIAE	PROGNOSTICATED	predicted
DIUELOPRN	PURLOINED	stolen
LRIGNKNA	RANKLING	irritating
PAERNUNCGE	REPUGNANCE	loathing
EECPTTRRSO	RETROSPECT	looking back on the past
IEESVERR	REVERIES	daydreams
SORUAUIBLS	SALUBRIOUS	healthful
ISNARGNUYA	SANGUINARY	sanguinary
TADETSIA	SATIATED	fully satisfied
EKLSDA	SLAKED	quenched
IPSSSOHM	SOPHISMS	misleading arguments
SNCUASNEET	SUSTENANCE	means of food or nourishment
OSTUIORM	TIMOROUS	fearful
CLVANGALTII	VACILLATING	fluctuating, wavering
AWNNLYOT	WANTONLY	immorally, cruelly
EWDCHETR	WRETCHED	miserable

www.ingramcontent.com/pod-product-compliance
Lightning Source LLC
Chambersburg PA
CBHW051415070526
44584CB00023B/3439